Reading Rules!

Motivating Teens to Read

Elizabeth Knowles

Martha Smith

2001
Libraries Unlimited, Inc.
And Its Division
Teacher Ideas Press
Englewood, Colorado

Libraries Unlimited, Inc.
And Its Division
Teacher Ideas Press
P.O. Box 6633
Englewood, CO 80155-6633
1-800-237-6124
www.lu.com

Library of Congress Cataloging-in-Publication Data

Knowles, Elizabeth, 1946-
    Reading rules! : motivating teens to read / Elizabeth Knowles, Martha Smith.
      p. cm.
    Includes bibliographical references.
    ISBN 1-56308-883-5 (pbk.)
     1. Teenagers--Books and reading. 2. Reading promotion. 3. Reading (Middle school)
4. Reading (Secondary) I. Smith, Martha, 1946- II. Title.

Z1037.A1 K58 2001
028.5'35--dc21

                                     2001029738

Reading Rules!

Contents

1

The Introduction/Situation

Teen Read Week, celebrated in the fall of each year and sponsored by the Young Adult Library Services Association, a division of the American Library Association, provides us with some very interesting facts about teens and reading:

- A growing number of teens can read but choose not to spend their free time reading.

- Reading skills become rusty when teens don't read books regularly.

- Teens will read more if they select what they want to read for their own enjoyment.

- Teens say they would read more if they had the time.

- Reading is a worthwhile experience that will last a lifetime.

- Knowledge of self and the world can be gained by reading.

- Few, if any, programs focus on literacy among teenagers.

   —2000 American Library Association (http://www.ala.org/teenread/ffacts.html)

In 1998 the National Assessment of Educational Programs administered the latest reading assessment to 31,000 students at grades 4, 8, and 12 in the nation and 360,000 students in individual states at grades 4 and 8. The assessment measured students' reading comprehension. The results of the report state:

- Fourth, eighth, and twelfth graders who reported reading the most pages daily—11 or more—for school and homework had the highest average reading scores.

- At all levels, students who reported talking about their reading activities with family or friends once or twice a week, or at least monthly, had higher average reading scores than students who reported doing so rarely or never.

- Students who reported watching three or fewer hours of television each day had higher average reading scores than those who reported watching more television.

▸▸ Only 5 percent of students surveyed in the 4th, 8th, and 12th grades performed at an advanced level; examining, extending, and elaborating on the meaning of literary and informative texts.

▸▸ Approximately 60 percent of the nation's adolescents can comprehend specific factual information, but few have gone beyond the basics to advanced reading and writing.

▸▸ Fewer than 5 percent of the nation's adolescents could extend or elaborate the meanings of the materials they read.

▸▸ Twenty-eight percent of 12th graders never read on their own for fun.

—U.S. Department of Education, Office of Educational Research and Improvement, National Center for Education Statistics. *NAEP 1998 Reading Report Card for the Nation* (Washington, D.C.: NCES, 1999: 459).

Stanley and Joy Steiner, in a March 1999 article in *Book Links*, state: "The number of people who cannot read or choose not to read is projected to reach 50% of the U.S. population by the year 2000. From recognizing print in the world around us to scanning the World Wide Web, we are a nation dependent on the ability to read, comprehend, and process large amounts of information."

These statistics show that once students complete the grades where reading is taught as a subject, either they are not skilled readers or they quickly change their attitudes toward reading and choose not to read. It seems that we are having difficulty producing students who have a lifelong love of reading. Many spend the rest of their time in school trying to get by and using any means to get through difficult, boring content area texts or required classic novels.

We have explored the many ways available to educators today to encourage middle school students to value reading. Each possible approach is examined in a separate chapter. The chapters may be used individually to promote an area where there is a need, or the entire book can be a tool to change the way teachers approach reading, either individually, by grade level, or in curriculum studies. We have annotated many professional books and included some of them in multiple chapters because the subject matter is broad and encompasses several areas. We have also included surveys for teachers and students so that you can evaluate right from the beginning.

Annotated Professional Journal Articles

Aronson, M. "When Coming of Age Meets the Age That's Coming: One Editor's View of How Young Adult Publishing Developed in America," *VOYA* (October 1998): 261-63.

Young adult literature is a fractured field. Teens are in an ambiguous middle ground. Parents no longer feel comfortable purchasing books for them. Teens do not appreciate adult suggestions but need guidance from librarians and teachers in selecting good fiction. They spend most of their money on music, clothes, sports, entertainment, and dates and don't have much left over for purchasing hardcover young adult books. Young adult fiction started as problem novels, but with television covering all the problems teens could possibly have, teen fiction lost its charm.

Aronson, M. "When Coming of Age Meets the Age That's Coming: One Editor's View of How Young Adult Publishing Developed in America, Part II: From YA Death Threat to New Teen Boom," *VOYA* (December 1998): 340-42.

Because young adult fiction was in a precarious position, publishers responded with series books and by changing the definition of young adult. *Sweet Valley High* began the most recent series explosion. Young adult now means an even lower age level than before because parents are pushing their children to read ahead, be ahead of their peers, and be ahead of their age level. There are more multicultural and poetry books for young adults available than ever before. Young adult fiction has ventured into many different areas in order to appeal to today's teens.

Campbell, P. "The Sand in the Oyster: Rescuing Young Adult Literature," *The Horn Book Magazine* (May/June 1997): 363-69.

Young adult fiction defies categorization because, like young adults themselves, it is constantly changing. Bookstores sell mostly young adult paperbacks while libraries want hardcover versions. YA hardcover is in trouble because of the rising cost of books and the diminishing funding of libraries. There are overlapping subcategories of ages within the broad category of young adult. All young adult titles now are read by middle school and younger students; high school readers are reading popular adult authors. This article suggests a Gen X category that would include fiction for the high school and early college age crowd. In this way young adult hardcover books might become popular again.

Muller, P. "Come On Down! Your Leadership Role in Advancing the National YA Agenda," *Journal of Youth Services in Libraries* (Winter 1999): 13-17.

Libraries should be taking advantage of goal setting and national standards to increase the attention given to the youth they serve. Teens should have the right to information that is developmentally appropriate and meets their needs for educational support, recreational interests, and leisure reading. They should encourage youth to take part in library planning, book and print material selection, and program planning. Teens can be effective spokespersons for their own needs. Teens should be actively involved in selecting the titles that appear on best-book lists for teens. They should serve on advisory boards and be part of web-site development. Libraries need to provide more popular magazines for teens.

Steiner, S. and J. "Navigating the Road to Literacy," *Book Links* (March 1999): 19-24.

Ensuring that all children and adults engage in the act of reading is a huge challenge for teachers, librarians, and parents when everyone is confronted with so many distractions. It is imperative that children have abundant role models for reading. People of all ages need access to books and other printed media. Environments need to be created at home and at school where talking about books is a natural way of life. Certainly book discussion groups are currently very popular. Some other successful approaches to encouraging reading include doctors prescribing reading to patients and stocking high-quality children's books in their waiting rooms; volunteers reading to children at community centers and homeless shelters; community groups providing gifts of books to new parents, homeless children and adults, and refugees; and schools rewarding students with books.

Annotated Professional Books

Booth, David. *Guiding the Reading Process: Techniques and Strategies for Successful Instruction in K-8 Classrooms.* Pembroke, 1998.

This is an exploration of the latest and most successful approaches to teaching reading. The book includes practical strategies and techniques to help students become successful, independent readers. This is an excellent resource for helping struggling readers of any age.

Hersch, Patricia. *A Tribe Apart: A Journey into the Heart of American Adolescence.* Ballantine, 1998.

For every day of an entire school year, Hersch shadowed eight teens through classes and activities to experience the realities of their lives. The most astonishing thing was that even the most supportive parents did not know about their teens' secret lives. Adults are simply not there as often as they should be—kids come home to empty houses or crippling responsibilities in caring for younger siblings. Families rarely eat together; extended families live far away. When teens do try to tell adults what is happening, they are often rejected and harshly judged. The conclusion is that every adolescent needs a mentor.

Leonhardt, Mary. *Keeping Kids Reading: How to Raise Avid Readers in the Video Age.* Three Rivers Press, 1996.

This is an important book for all parents and teachers. It is easy to read and has many practical suggestions for getting kids to read and keeping them on reading paths. It has goals, strategies, tips, and help for getting kids to write for pleasure and looks at educational goals, dealing with homework, and tips and strategies for teenagers.

2

The Problem

What has happened in our schools and homes across the nation to create so many teens who can read but choose not to? According to Beers (1996) there are three voices of aliteracy. One is dormant, the students who say that they would read but just don't have the time right now—there is too much going on to take time to sit and read a book just for the fun of it. There are also the uncommitted readers who think they might read sometime in the future. The third kind are the unmotivated readers who just plain refuse to read, saying they know they are not going to enjoy it anyway, so why bother.

In an article in the March 1997 issue of the *English Journal*, Jim Cope questioned high school seniors about their reading. He found that many of the strongest reading memories of these students were negative, and the students related school reading experiences that turned them off. He calls their fear of assigned reading Moby-phobia. The works of one author came under the most fire: Shakespeare. Alan Purves points out that Shakespeare's plays were meant to be seen and heard, not read and dissected. Much of the imagery and dialogue in the plays rushed by the audience so that it was the drift, not each individual segment, that was the focus. Students were further turned off by spending too long on one particular work or on overanalysis. Other things students disliked were book reports and having to read aloud. Cope ends the article, "Students learn more from things they understand and want to read rather than when they are being forced to read something of no interest to them."

In many middle school literature classes the students are reading classic novels, and the lessons are teacher-directed with vocabulary lists, literal comprehension questions, and the students listening to the teacher tell them what they should be "getting" from their readings. No connections are made to the way things are today, and no connections are made to young adult literature. In fact, English/literature teachers feel that young adult novels are not good enough to be included in the curriculum.

In content area classes the texts are often difficult and boring, written by experts in the field in a style that makes comprehension a challenge. In most classes no connections are made to nonfiction trade books, nor are there any reading strategies taught to help students comprehend. Most content area teachers feel they are not trained to teach reading; that should have been taken care of in the lower grades.

Not many teachers and librarians spend much time booktalking young adult titles in order to persuade or entice students to read. Most teachers are very busy trying to cover material, so that no block of time is ever given in class for uninterrupted, student-selected reading. And certainly, most teachers are looking for the correct answer to the comprehension question, and no one is asking the students what they think about the book, how they feel about the characters, and so forth.

▣ **Survey Questions about Current Reading Program**

1. Is our current reading program meeting the needs of the young adolescent students?

2. Is it instilling the love of reading and creating young adults who will become lifelong readers?

3. Is there a special place in the media center for young adults? Are current young adult titles and magazines available?

4. Are there comfortable places to read in classrooms and a selection of young adult titles available for student selection?

5. Does our faculty value young adults' opinions about their reading?

6. Do literature classes require the reading of classics with literal comprehension questions and correct answers based only on the teacher's interpretation of the classic?

7. Do we allow young adults time to read during the school day?

8. Do we allow them to select their reading material?

9. Do we "sell" young adult literature through displays and booktalks?

10. Do we offer multiple opportunities for young adults to meet together in clubs or groups to discuss current literature?

11. Can our students read and comprehend their content area texts?

12. Are teachers complaining that students can't or won't read content area texts?

13. Are students enthusiastic about reading?

14. Are students overwhelmed when it comes to the Internet and research?

Annotated Professional Journal Articles

Beers, G. Kylene. "No Time, No Interest, No Way! The 3 Voices of Aliteracy, Part 1," *School Library Journal* (February 1996): 30-33.

The group of students who can read but won't is growing. There are three types of aliterate readers: dormant, uncommitted, and unmotivated. Dormant readers are those who like to read but are so busy that they don't have time to read. If the conditions are right they will read.

Uncommitted readers do not like to read. They view it as a skill; however, they may choose to read in the future. Unmotivated readers also view reading as a skill, but they do not plan to be readers in the future. Reading is boring, nothing happens. Aliterates have many differing views "about themselves, about others, and about reading. By understanding those views, we can come closer to understanding why some students choose not to read."

Beers, G. Kylene. "No Time, No Interest, No Way! The 3 Voices of Aliteracy, Part 2," *School Library Journal* (March 1996): 110-13.

This is part two of an article about three types of aliteracy: dormant, uncommitted, and unmotivated. All three types of aliterate students had varied experiences with books in their early childhood. The dormant reader remembers being read to on a regular basis. The uncommitted and unmotivated readers were read to infrequently, and it was never a form of entertainment.

The dormant readers had library cards, went to story times, and joined the summer reading clubs, whereas the other students who later did not value reading never had these positive, pleasurable experiences. Different techniques and tips for motivating dormant students versus the uncommitted and unmotivated are listed. The sooner one can reach these aliterate students, the more likely one can initiate change.

Bushman, John H. "Young Adult Literature in the Classroom—Or Is It?" *English Journal* (March 1997): 35-40.

Do the classics meet the needs, interests, and abilities of our young people today? The author believes the classics meet the intellectual requirements of students, but are they appropriate for seventh and eighth graders? Young adults are primarily interested in their social and emotional development. Therefore we should use current YA literature to stimulate our students and speak to their issues.

The author sent a questionnaire to students in grades 6 through 12 concerning several aspects of reading both in and out of school. The results show that, the older they get, the less students read for pleasure outside of school. We are introducing the classics at an earlier age and not introducing students to authors they will read. Teachers are interested in teaching curriculum but are not encouraging students to become lifelong readers. We have students who are aliterate, "people who are able to read and write but choose not to use these skills very often. Teachers must turn kids on to reading instead of turning them off."

Carroll, Pamela Sissi. "Today's Teen, Their Problems, and Their Literature: Revisiting G. Robert Carlsen's *Books and the Teenage Reader* Thirty Years Later," *English Journal* (March 1997): 25-34.

The author looks at Carlsen's 1967 edition of *Books and the Teenage Reader* to see if the reasons teenagers read and do not read more still apply. Children work through emotional, social, cognitive, and spiritual tasks on their path to adulthood, and we must provide YA literature to help them in this process.

Several myths were debunked regarding teens, and the author discusses eight of the most serious problems those teens face as compared to 1967. As teachers and media specialists we must examine these books for their accuracy and continually update our lists of suggested and classroom readings.

Cope, Jim. "Beyond Voices of Readers: Students on School's Effects on Reading," *English Journal* (March 1997): 18-23.

    The author asks students to relate their positive and negative experiences about reading. At the top of the list of negative experiences was the assigned reading of books students could not relate to, followed by books and plays of Dickens or Shakespeare. We are presenting good literature at the wrong time. We should be using YA literature in middle school, saving the classics for when students are developmentally ready. Students did not like the methods used to teach literature. Teachers would overanalyze and look for symbolism until reading was no longer pleasurable. Book reports were third in the list of negative reading experiences, followed by reading aloud. On the positive side, students liked to have choices in their reading and being read aloud to. We must have confidence in our students to choose books that will lead them to read more often.

Humphrey, Jack W. "Learning Not to Read" *Education Week* (March 2000): 43-44.

    There was a period when reading classes were eliminated, and that class time was used to learn a foreign language or computers. It is time to reverse that trend and provide reading classes and instruction. Included are the reading teacher's classroom, schoolwide, community, and professional goals and expectations.

Reid, Louann, and Ruth K. J. Cline. "Our Repressed Reading Addictions: Teachers and Young Adult Series Books," *English Journal* (March 1997): 68-72.

    Series books deserve a place in our classrooms and libraries. They are popular because the plots are exciting and move along quickly, yet they are safe and written to a formula. The text is familiar and the titles are readily available. Students like to share and talk about series books. Students who enjoy series books will eventually move on to other titles. Because these encourage reading, we should have them accessible.

3

The Solutions

This chapter discusses the solutions that are available for changing the attitudes of unmotivated young adult readers. These solutions bring about positive adjustments in the reading habits of middle level students and in the attitudes of teachers. The following chapters will identify a variety of ways teachers can improve the attitudes and skills of middle level students when it comes to reading. Each chapter may be used as a separate informational document on that topic. There will be a research-based description, discussion questions for use among professionals, practical application, annotated journal articles and professional books, and sample young adult titles. This will provide in-service information on ways teachers can conduct literature classes, and support for these changes for decision makers such as principals and school boards. This book could form the basis for a reading council to make changes in the school's reading program.

The solutions include literature circles, readers' workshops, booktalks, book clubs, improving the reading environment, thematic/interdisciplinary units, current young adult literature, reading in the content areas, information literacy, research and report writing, and an overall school reading plan for middle grade students.

Literature circles provide the opportunity for students to select a book, read, and then discuss the book with a group of classmates. The students can all read the same book, they can read the same author, or they can read on a particular topic or subject. The participants in literature circles usually have a job to carry out as a member of the group. There are always open-ended questions available to spark discussion. Students are requested to keep a journal of their reactions to the story as they read. The teacher can require a culminating activity for the group.

Readers' workshop is a way of teaching reading all year long. It includes student selection choice, plenty of class time to read, a required response journal, regular conference time with the teacher, flexible discussion groups, and lots of mini-lessons. The mini-lessons cover skills and literary concepts but can be done in a number of ways—whole class, small group, pairs, or individuals—and usually are need-based.

Booktalks are advertisements for books. The librarian, a teacher, or a student can present booktalks. There can be props, but they are not necessary. They can be prepared and rehearsed or given on the spur of the moment. A character, an event, or the theme might be described, but the ending of the story is never shared. The purpose is to entice the other students to read the book.

Oprah Winfrey has made book clubs popular. There can be book clubs for girls, boys, teachers, parents, mothers and daughters, fathers and sons, students by grade level—any grouping is possible. The purpose is to get together and discuss a book that all group members have read on their own time. It helps everyone understand that a story can mean different things to different people, and we each bring our own set of interests, experiences, and knowledge when we read.

The reading environment is a very important part of encouraging middle level reading. The students have to feel safe, comfortable, and free from criticism and threats. There should be a special place for them to read in the media center as well as in their classrooms. The school should demonstrate the importance of reading by having schoolwide reading times and administrators and faculty who read aloud to middle level students. There should be a great variety of reading materials available all over the school. Students should be made to feel that their opinions about books are valued, and that they are an important part of any book discussion group.

It is important to bring the faculty along on this crusade to turn middle level students into lifelong readers. Thematic or interdisciplinary teaching with literature as the basis for topic study will help students discover the wide variety of books available on any topic. It is necessary to bring young adult literature into the curriculum so that students can see similarities between classics and history and modern-day times.

Books presented in class tend to be the classics and textbooks, but faculty must be aware of the many excellent young adult titles available each year. Teachers and librarians need to keep up with these titles and include other teachers in the reading of these books so that they can be added to the curriculum. Students are more apt to identify with character types, situations, and settings with which they are familiar. YA books can bridge the gap between curriculum and the students' interests. The recent addition of a young adult award by the ALA is an important step toward giving current young adult authors the acclaim they are due.

Students must be supported in their efforts to read in the content areas. Very often students are stuck with a difficult, boring textbook. It is important that content area teachers provide connections to literature—picture books, historical fiction, nonfiction, biographies, and science fiction—so students can see that there are many ways to explore content area subjects.

The Internet has provided today's students with more information than they can handle. They often find information on the Internet but then do not know if it is accurate, current, biased, or how to read through it to extract the facts they need. Reading is more important than ever when students are faced with screen after screen of print. The tendency is just to print it all, or to copy and paste parts into a document for class. Students need to learn a research process for using the Web.

This leads us to a reading plan, filled with strategies to encourage middle level students to become lifelong readers. It is an action plan that will involve all adults and the students themselves. It does not require much financial backing—just some focus on the needs of middle level students and help for them to become confident and responsive readers of all types of literature.

Annotated Professional Journal Article

Ivey, G. "Redesigning Reading Instruction," *Educational Leadership* (September 2000): 42-45.

One-size instruction never really fit anyone. Low level readers spend their schools days getting fragmented skill instruction but hardly any time to read and write. Round-robin reading does little to develop reading skills and engage individual students. Newly marketed teacher resources for novels have all students in the class reading the same book and spending excessive amounts of time on "bells and whistles" activities, worksheets, quizzes, and comprehension questions. There is little time to actually read; schools should allow time to read every day. More resources should be allocated for a wide variety of reading materials, and students should have input on the selection.

Annotated Professional Books

Herz, S. *From Hinton to Hamlet: Building Bridges between Young Adult Literature and the Classics.* Greenwood Press, 1996.

The value of young adult literature lies in its ability to draw students' attention into the story immediately because it deals with real problems in their own lives. Young adult literature gives students the right to experience reading as a pleasurable activity and helps them to become competent readers. These are some of the unique characteristics of young adult literature: the main character is a teenager; the events, problems, and plots are related to teens; the dialogue reflects teenage speech; the point of view is from an adolescent's perspective; the novel is short; and the actions and decisions of the main characters are major factors in the outcome of the conflict. This book suggests that young adult literature should be an important part of literature classes; it can be used as a bridge to the classics.

Moeller, M. and V. *Middle School English Teacher's Guide to Active Learning.* Eye on Education, 2000.

This book begins with a discussion of two models of teaching: the didactic and the Socratic. It continues with a discussion of active and close reading—the purpose of which is learning to read, interpret or pay attention to not only what the author has to say but also how it is said. What does the book say? What does it mean? Is it true? There are three kinds of questions: factual, interpretive, and evaluation. The theory behind active learning is discussed, and sample lessons include questions on various books, including *The Chocolate War, The Giver, Of Mice and Men,* and *The Little Prince.*

Pennac, Daniel. *Better than Life.* Stenhouse/Pembroke, 1999.

This book contains the Readers Bill of Rights. The author explores simple ways to create a lifelong devotion to reading.

4

The Reading Environment

Elementary classrooms and libraries entice children to read with attractive bulletin boards, reading lofts, book nooks, pillows, comfortable furniture, displays with stuffed animals, and brightly colored plastic crates of fun things to read. Yet middle level readers usually do not have a place to call their own in the library. Classrooms are more functional for traveling teachers, short class periods, and content area subjects. By the time students reach upper-middle levels, the environment is less attractive and less conducive to escaping to a corner with a good book. Teachers in the elementary grades entice children by reading aloud frequently; middle level teachers are trying to cover curriculum and prepare students for the next level in their content area—there is no time to read a good book aloud.

Current research indicates that creating spaces for adolescents is very important. They need to have a place to call their own: in the library, in the classrooms, and on the school's web site. It is up to the adults who work with adolescents to create spaces and environments conducive to reading, reflecting, and discussing. It is also important to let adolescents know that their opinions and feelings about their reading are valued. It is also important to involve them in the decision-making process—to create an advisory panel for the library, to create a team to develop their special portion of the school's web site, and to have their input in the selection of reading materials for the library and classrooms.

Efforts should be made to develop a survey to find out what the middle level students like to read and what their interests are. Based on the survey results, evaluate and upgrade the books available to adolescents in the library and in the classroom. Try an attention-getting program—something splashy like a Murder Mystery Party with refreshments, favors, and decorations. Actively involve all middle level teachers and administration in the crucial effort to place a schoolwide focus on adolescent reading.

Professional Discussion Questions

1. Do we have a special space for adolescents in our library? If not, how could we accomplish this?

2. Do we have an adolescent advisory panel for the library to help select materials and maintain the space?

3. Do we ask adolescents to review books and post those reviews on the web site or on a bulletin board or computer database in the library?

4. Do we encourage adolescents to respond to literature in the classroom with reflection and discussion?

5. What can we do to provide our adolescent students with a reading environment in our school?

6. How do we get teachers in the content areas to include reading in their curriculum?

Practical Application

Brain-Centered Environment Basics

This list, from Eric Jensen's six-day brain compatible learning workshop, "How the Brain Learns" in San Diego, California, in March 2000, shows how to create a brain-friendly environment for learning.

1. Seating—no longer than 10 minutes in seat (soon postural stress becomes greater than learning).

2. Music—approximately 15 percent of class time.

3. Posters and peripherals—content, student work, symbolic, affirmations, pre-exposure, preaching.

4. Lighting—brighter is better, natural is better.

5. Color—paint rooms light gray, yellow, or orange. Use bright color in instruction, for note taking, and for mind mapping.

6. Temperature—68 to 70 degrees Fahrenheit.

7. Plants—real plants in every classroom: rubber, palms, spider, ficus, dracaena.

8. Water—should be available all the time: children should be encouraged to drink.

9. Manipulatives—very important in all subject areas.

10. Rate of change—every two to four weeks; students should be making the changes: bulletin boards, wall decorations, posters, displays, and room arrangement.

Middle School Media Center Advisory Panel

Two students from each grade level meet regularly to maintain a young adult place in the media center and help in the selection of books and magazines. They should review titles and post reviews on the media center's web page and then rate the books and produce a list of best books for the school year. Planning and leading book discussion groups, special parties and activities, and brainstorming ideas for getting fellow middle school students to read for pleasure should also be part of the group's responsibilities.

Checklist for Evaluating the Media Center

1. Area set aside for quiet reading

2. Area set aside for casual reading

3. Alternative seating arrangements: rocking chairs, pillows, etc.

4. Reading areas defined with rugs or furniture arrangements

5. Easy-to-read and highly visible signage

6. Works of art displayed, preferably students'

7. Displays for books

8. Displays for magazines

9. Displays for paperbacks, pamphlets, and brochures

10. Bulletin boards for news, upcoming events, and promoting reading

11. Posters that encourage reading

12. Variety of books that spark the students' interest

13. Displays changed every two weeks

14. Bulletin boards changed monthly

15. Attractive plants throughout the center

16. Use of attractive colors throughout the center

17. Natural lighting and full-spectrum lighting rather than cool-white fluorescent

18. Colorful displays based on curriculum or themes

Sample Curriculum Displays

▣ Social Studies

◀◀ Books about countries

◀◀ Globes

◀◀ Flags from other countries

◀◀ Maps, puzzle maps, large floor maps

◀◀ Fiction books that use that area or time period as the setting

◀◀ Artifacts, primary documents

◀◀ Picture books about social studies

◀◀ Pamphlet/bookmark of web sites, books, AV materials available

▣ **Science**

- ◂◂ Manipulatives, working models
- ◂◂ Pop-up science books
- ◂◂ Subject-oriented nonfiction books
- ◂◂ Magnets, magnifying glass
- ◂◂ Aquarium, terrarium
- ◂◂ Telescope
- ◂◂ Compass, collections of rocks, shells, etc.
- ◂◂ Picture books about science
- ◂◂ Pamphlet/bookmark of web sites, books, AV materials available

▣ **Math**

- ◂◂ Manipulatives
- ◂◂ Triangles, abacus
- ◂◂ Puzzles
- ◂◂ Nonfiction and fiction books about math
- ◂◂ Picture books about math
- ◂◂ Height chart
- ◂◂ Pamphlet/bookmark of web sites, books, AV materials available

▣ **Music**

- ◂◂ Books about composers, famous musicians
- ◂◂ Books about instruments and types of music
- ◂◂ CD with headphones to coincide with display
- ◂◂ Actual instruments
- ◂◂ Pamphlet/bookmark of web sites, books, AV materials available

▣ **Art**

- ◂◂ Books about artists and types of art
- ◂◂ Origami books and paper
- ◂◂ Art calendars
- ◂◂ Posters of real art
- ◂◂ Pamphlet/bookmark of web sites, books, AV materials available

▣ **Cross-Curriculum**

Make a display using a theme that incorporates several subjects.

Reader's Survey

◀◀ How would you describe yourself as a reader?

◀◀ Do you find some kinds of material harder to read than others? If so, what? What makes it harder?

◀◀ Do you discuss the books you have read with other students or friends?

◀◀ Do you like to read?

◀◀ When and where do you read?

◀◀ Do you buy books to read?

◀◀ Do you subscribe to any magazines at home? If so what are they?

◀◀ Do you read any magazines or newspapers on a regular basis? If so what?

◀◀ What do you like to read?

| Comic books | Magazines | Books |

◀◀ What is your favorite type of book to read? (Circle all that apply.)

Fiction	Nonfiction	Biography
Humorous	Historical fiction	Mystery
Science fiction	Fantasy	Realistic
Classics	Sports	Adventure

◀◀ Do you use the public library? (Circle all that apply.)

| All the time | Once in awhile | Never |

◀◀ If you go to the public library, what do you do? (Circle all that apply.)

| Borrow books | Homework | Research |

◀◀ Do you use your school library?   YES   NO   When do you use the library?

◀◀ What do you like best about your school library?

◀◀ What would you like to change in your school library?

◀◀ I am able to locate materials in the school library

| Easily | With some difficulty | Never |

◂◂ If your library has a web site, how often do you go to it?

   All the time   Occasionally   Never

◂◂ I prefer   thin / thick   books. (Circle one.)

◂◂ Do you ever use audio books?   YES   NO

◂◂ Do you like to get books that are recommended by a friend?   YES   NO

◂◂ Do you choose a book based on its cover?   YES   NO

◂◂ Do you choose a book by an author you are familiar with?   YES   NO

◂◂ Do you choose a book based on the jacket blurbs?   YES   NO

◂◂ Who is your favorite author?

◂◂ What is your favorite subject?

◂◂ Are you aware of new books when they come into your library?   YES   NO

◂◂ Does your library accept suggestions for new acquisitions?

   YES   NO   DON'T KNOW

◂◂ Do you have a computer at home?   YES   NO   If yes, how much time do you spend on the computer each day?

◂◂ How much television do you watch a day?

◂◂ What are your favorite television shows?

◂◂ Do you have a book collection at home?

Teacher's Survey

◂◂ Would you like to participate with the library using information and technology in joint projects?

◂◂ Are you satisfied with the way your students use the library? If yes, what is it that you like? If no, what would you like to do differently?

◂◂ What additional services would you like the library to provide?

◂◂ Do you think that reading incentive programs are worthwhile for your students?

◂◂ Do you think we should require students to read a certain number of books or pages each semester?

◂◂ Do you think we should have required summer reading?

◂◂ Would you like to see DEAR (Drop Everything and Read) day adopted schoolwide?

◂◂ Are you satisfied with your reading program?

◀◀ Would you like assistance from the library in setting up literature circles in your classroom?

Annotated Professional Journal Articles

Johnson, Doug. "No More Agents of Benevolent Neglect!" *The Book Report* (January/February 1996): 22-23.

This article contains a very thorough 12-point library media program checklist with an excellent emphasis on media technology. The media center is a critical element in creating a positive reading environment for adolescents.

Jones, Patrick. "A Cyber-Room of Their Own: How Libraries Use Web Pages to Attract Young Adults," *School Library Journal* (November 1997): 34-37.

This article describes how young adults not only need a physical space of their own in a library, they also need a special section just for teens within the library's or school's web site.

Kelly, Deirdre. "Brain-Based Learning.com," *Classroom Connect* (May 2000): 16-17.

This article highlights how important it is for teachers to be aware of basic brain functions in adolescents. For instance, it is advisable to put test-phobic students at ease, because if you don't, the emotional part of their brains will get all their energy and the cerebral part (thinking and reasoning) will not function at its best level. The article provides information about 13 brain web sites for teachers and students.

Lowe, Jeff. "Creating an A+++ Classroom Library," *Instructor* (August 1998): 61-63.

The author shares a foolproof system for setting up a classroom library where students will beg for silent reading time. He shares ideas on how to acquire books: book clubs; students donating books in the names of friends, parents, pets, and special occasions; and soliciting donations of old books from students and the community. He also gives advice about shelving, location, displays, and record keeping.

National Middle School Association. "Creating a Positive Classroom," *Classroom Connections* (April 2000): 1-2.

This article, geared specifically toward middle school educators, shares ideas on creating a positive classroom environment for adolescents. It includes a quick quiz for teachers, great practical suggestions for creating a welcoming room, pointers for teachers as role models, effective disciplinary techniques, and a list of "lifesavers."

Vidor, Constance. "The Castle Comes of Age: Attracting Young Adults to a K-8 Library," *School Library Journal* (October 1997): 24-27.

The librarian at the Cathedral School of the Cathedral of St. John the Divine in New York City shares her quest to develop a young adult collection and a special space for adolescents to read in a library dominated by younger kids and little furniture. Once the collection and the space was established, she describes how she got the middle level kids to use the library and share their interest in the new books.

VOYA column, YA "Spaces of Your Dreams."

Each issue of *VOYA* has a guest writer for the "Spaces of Your Dreams" column. Librarians share how they created special spaces and atmospheres for teens, and how they get adolescents involved with books, magazines, and technology in new and exciting ways.

Williams, Mary. "Bookmarking Your Library's Teens," *VOYA* (August 1999): 172-73.

This article shares an idea of photographing teens reading in the library and then turning those photos into bookmarks in order to help spread the word about teen reading.

Annotated Professional Books

Barrett, Susan. *It's All in Your Head: A Guide to Understanding Your Brain and Boosting Your Brain Power.* Free Spirit, 1992.

In this book you will discover how the brain evolved, what the different parts do, the trouble with IQ tests, how many different intelligences you have, what makes a person a genius, why play is good for your brain, 10 tips for making life easier, 20 ways to become more creative than you already are, mysteries of the mind, and much more. It is easy to read, clear, and straightforward—and provides everything your students need to know about their brains and how they work.

Jensen, Eric. *Completing the Puzzle: The Brain-Compatible Approach to Learning—A Research Based Guide to Implementing the Dramatic New Learning Paradigms.* The Brain Store, 1997.

Recent discoveries in neuroscience, physics, and systems theory now give you powerful strategies for educational success. Brain-compatible learning is dynamic, interdisciplinary, and systemwide. Explore these topics in this book: rain forests and the human brain, instructional strategies, environment, curriculum, assessment, organizational approaches, and the future.

Jensen, Eric. *Introduction to Brain-Compatible Learning.* The Brain Store, 1998.

Explore these topics: what is brain-compatible learning, where's the proof, why should we care about the research, fun factoids about the brain, brain biology 101, right and left hemispheres, facts about brain cells, boys' and girls' brains, developmental stages of readiness, brain-smart classrooms, emotions and learning, mind-body learning, attention and learning, chemistry of behavior, feeding the brain, the up side of down time, nonconscious learning, the adaptive brain, boosting motivation, avoiding rewards, and much more!

Jensen, Eric. *Teaching with the Brain in Mind.* Association for Supervision and Curriculum Development, 1998.

Included are the latest practical, easy-to-understand research on learning and the brain, how to balance the research and theory, and successful tips and techniques for use in the classroom. There are in-depth discussions of emotion, memory, and recall. This book is concise, accessible, and informative.

Morrow, Lesley Mandel. *The Literacy Center.* Stenhouse Publishers, 1997.

This is a practical book with many ideas on motivating children to become independent readers and writers through the sixth grade. The book is divided into five chapters that include motivating reading and writing, designing a literacy center, modeling literature activities, the organization, management, and assessment, and scenes from the literacy center. The remainder of the book is devoted to resources. Although much of the book is geared to younger children, the beginning chapters are helpful if you are establishing a literacy center environment.

Sousa, David. *How the Brain Learns: A Classroom Teacher's Guide.* National Association of Secondary School Principals, 1995.

Dr. Sousa explores the new research and its implications for educators. The book begins with basic brain facts and how the brain processes information. It continues by discussing memory, retention, learning and the power of transfer, left/right brain processing, thinking skills and learning, and then putting it all together.

Sprenger, Marilee. *Learning & Memory: The Brain in Action.* Association for Supervision and Curriculum Development, 1999.

Chapters in this book include: losing your mind—the function of brain cells; chicken soup for the brain—the effects of brain chemicals; pieces and parts—brain anatomy, memory and storage systems, locating memories, instructional strategies for using memory, assessment that mirrors instructional strategies, and FAQs.

Sylwester, Robert. *A Celebration of Neurons: An Educator's Guide to the Human Brain.* Association for Supervision and Curriculum Development, 1995.

This book for educators gives an introduction to the brain so that you can identify parts of the brain, discuss scientists' theories about how the brain functions, how it interacts with the environment, how it solves problems, and how it learns, remembers, and forgets. The book is an urgent call for educators to become more involved in useful applications for brain theory and research in the classroom.

Web Sites

The Brain Connection
http://www.brainconnection.com

The Brain Lab
http://www.newhorizons.org/blab.html

Exploratorium: The Memory Exhibition
http://www.exploratorium.edu/memory/index.html

Graphic Organizer Index
http://www.graphic.org/goindex.html

The Learning Brain Newsletter
http://www.learningbrain.com/

Neuroscience for Kids
    http://faculty.washington.edu/chudler/neurok.html

A Science Odyssey: Probe the Brain
    http://www.pbs.org/wgbh/aso/tryit/brain/

The Whole Brain Atlas
    http://www.med.harvard.edu/AANLIB/home.html

5

Reading Workshop

Nancie Atwell has written about reading workshop, and it is supported by The National Council of Teachers of English and others in the field of reading. According to Calkins (2000) the actual reading time is the most important part of reading workshop. Muschla (1997) says there are many kinds of reading classes, but what sets the reading workshop apart is its emphasis on reading. Atwell (1998) sets up a reading workshop in the classroom with approximately 1,000 paperbacks arranged alphabetically by author's last name. Students rate books from 1 to 10 as they read, and at the end of the school year each class puts together a best-book list from their ratings.

The most important aspect of reading workshop is that reading is paramount, respected, and celebrated. Sufficient time must be allowed for adolescents to "get into" a book. A wide variety of books on a number of levels should be available, and students should be able to choose what they want to read. Reading skills are taught on an as-needed basis in the format called mini-lessons, which may be taught to the whole class, a small group of students, or an individual. Students are encouraged to keep a reading log of titles read. It is okay not to finish a book, and the title and the reasons why the book was abandoned should be noted in the reading log. A reading response journal should also be kept to record daily observations and feelings about students' readings. Reading and writing go together in the reading workshop classroom.

The workshop format offers structure but remains flexible, with most of the time set aside for student reading. Some teachers prefer to use a contract for each book the students read; one example is SOS: summary, opinion, and support (of the opinion). The best part of the reading workshop format is that it allows the teacher to have a one-on-one conference time with each student every week.

Responding to literature, especially in written format, is an important part of reading workshop. There are many factors that affect responses: cognitive development, experience, language development, the text, the context, classroom atmosphere, and teachers' attitudes.

Instead of absorbing an elusive "one right meaning" from a text, readers rely on their own background knowledge and create unique meanings, according to Rosenblatt (1978). Who is reading, what is being read, the purposes for reading, and the social and cultural factors surrounding reading all influence what a particular reader creates while reading a particular text. Responses are influenced by many factors and come in many forms. Children who have many experiences with books bring a wealth of knowledge to the texts they read.

Three principles guide our discussion of language and literature. First, children develop language naturally as they interact with language users. Second, we also know that in language development comprehension generally exceeds language production. Third, language learning never ends. As students mature, language skills increase and awareness grows in direct proportion to experiences.

It is vital to understand at least three things about the social nature of reading and responding to literature. First, learning occurs in a social context that is dependent on interaction; literature plays an important role in that context. Second, children grow in their ability to understand literature as they gain experience with life and literature. Third, a teacher's influence on a child's response to literature is very powerful. There are many ways to respond: by laughter and applause; browsing or focused attention on books; sharing; reading together; storytelling and discussion; dramatic play; drawings and displays; and summarizing, and writing about literature.

Professional Discussion Questions

1. How can we get teachers involved in reading current young adult fiction?

2. Is it necessary for the teacher to have read all the books available in the classroom?

3. What methods can teachers use to assess student comprehension other than literal comprehension questions?

4. What should the teacher be doing while the students read?

5. How can the teacher be sure that the students are reading on or above level and growing in their reading and comprehension?

6. What should a teacher do when a student seems unable to write about what has been read?

7. How does the teacher schedule and monitor discussion groups, and how are the groups formed?

8. How does a teacher grade reading workshop?

Practical Application

Sample Mini-Lesson Topics

▣ **Some Suggestions for Response Journal Writing**

  ◂◂ What you liked or disliked and why

  ◂◂ What you wish had happened

  ◂◂ What you wish the author had included

  ◂◂ Your opinion of the characters

◀◀ Your opinion of the illustrations

◀◀ What the story reminds you of

◀◀ What you felt as you read

◀◀ What you noticed about how you read

◀◀ Questions you have after reading

▣ Possible Mini-Lessons

◀◀ How to give a booktalk

◀◀ Differences between fiction and nonfiction

◀◀ Books written in the first, second, or third person

◀◀ Author studies

◀◀ Story setting

◀◀ Characterization

◀◀ Problem/event/solution pattern

◀◀ Similes and metaphors

◀◀ Foreshadowing

◀◀ Selecting response topics

◀◀ Figuring out unknown words

◀◀ Making predictions

◀◀ Mapping a story

◀◀ Deciding on the theme of the story

◀◀ Making inferences

◀◀ Drawing conclusions

◀◀ Distinguishing fact from opinion

◀◀ Summarizing a story

◀◀ Skimming/speed reading

◀◀ Compare/contrast

◀◀ Dialogue

◀◀ Interviewing

◀◀ Note taking

◀◀ Paraphrasing

◀◀ A study strategy

- ◂◂ A comprehension strategy

- ◂◂ Proofreading/revising

- ◂◂ Topic sentences/main idea

- ◂◂ Characterization

▣ **Sample Questions to Start Discussions**

- ◂◂ What do you think of this book?

- ◂◂ What's this book about?

- ◂◂ What were you wondering about as you read this book?

- ◂◂ If you had a chance to speak with this author, what questions would you ask?

- ◂◂ Why do you suppose the author gave the book this title?

- ◂◂ Have you ever read other books by this author? If so, are the other books like this one?

- ◂◂ If you could be like any character in the book, who would you be like and why?

- ◂◂ Does this book remind you of any other books you have read? If so, which ones?

- ◂◂ If this story took place somewhere else or in a different time, how would it be different?

- ◂◂ Tell us a little bit about your favorite part of the story.

- ◂◂ Why did you choose this book?

- ◂◂ Are you like anyone in this book? If so, who?

- ◂◂ What do you think is going to happen next and why?

- ◂◂ To whom would you recommend this book and why?

Annotated Young Adult Literature

Calabro, Marian. *The Perilous Journey of the Donner Party.* Clarion Books, 1999.

Life was good for the well-off Donner and Reed families in Springfield, Illinois. The prospect of large tracts of land in California 2,500 miles away was greater. They packed up all they owned and left on April 15, 1846. They joined with another group, and it eventually totaled 87 people. Under the influence of James Reed they took the Hastings Cutoff, which was supposed to shorten the journey by 300 miles. The trail was nonexistent, so they cut a wagon trail through the Wasatch Range in Utah. Instead of covering 12 to 15 miles per day, they only covered 2 to 5 miles. As a result, they reached the Sierra Nevada summit, Truckee Lake (now Donner Lake), in late October. They were unable to cross the summit due to weather, hunger, and fatigue, and 81 people were forced to make camp at Truckee Lake and try to survive the winter until help came. They were desperate people and took desperate measures to survive. Virginia Reed, age 13, wrote later to her cousin: "O Mary I have not rote you half of the truble we have had but I have rote you anuf to let you now that you don't know what truble is . . . don't let this letter dishaten (dishearten) anybody never take no cut-offs and hury along as fast as you can." Forty-seven survivors reached California.

Haddix, Margaret Peterson. *Among the Hidden.* Simon & Schuster Books for Young Readers, 1998.

Watch out for the Population Police! This society passed the Population Law after terrible droughts and rationing in an overpopulated world. "They wanted to make sure there would never be more people than the farmer could feed." Therefore only two children are allowed per family. A third child is a shadow child, hidden and sometimes mistreated, starved, abused—even murdered.

Luke spends most of his days in the attic of his house avoiding all windows, peering out of a covered vent. One day he sees a face, a shadow child named Jen, at a neighboring house. Luke breaks all rules and secretly visits Jen when he dares. Jen has access to a computer and is planning a rally of "thirds" to come out of hiding and show themselves to the world at the president's house. Will Jen change the course of history and free the hidden? What part, if any, will Luke play?

Howe, James. *The Watcher.* Aladdin Paperbacks, 1997.

Summer on Fire Island, a lifeguard, a family, and a lonely girl who sits on the steps and watches everything but does not speak, join in, or go in the water. She makes up stories about how she is part of an imaginary family. Eventually, she goes into one of the summer cottages and takes a family picture and a few other things. The boy in the family discovers that she has taken the things, and in going to confront her, he comes upon a frightening scene.

Levitin, Sonia. *The Cure.* Silver Whistle, 1999.

It is the year 2407 and Gemm16884 has just experienced that dream again. Even when he was young, Gemm knew that he was different because he loved music, rhythms, and singing. Because diversity is evil in the eyes of the elders, Gemm is offered a chance to redeem himself. He must partake in the Cure. Gemm agrees, and he returns to an age when music and love offset the evil and squalor. Gemm becomes Johannes, a Jew living in Strasbourg, Germany. It is the time of the black plague, 1348. As the plague spreads throughout Europe, the Jews are blamed for it, and terror and evil reign. Johannes and his community suffer and die, and Gemm returns to the futuristic society allegedly cured. Gemm knows that "diversity can lead to emotions—and emotions can bring us either to hatred or love. People must have that choice." Will it begin again with Gemm?

McNeal, Laura and Tom. *Crooked.* Alfred A. Knopf, 1999.

Ninth graders Clara and Amos find their lives at home in shambles as they try to develop a romance. Amos witnesses two local hoodlum brothers destroying property, and they try to silence Amos by hitting him with a baseball bat. He becomes a hero to his friends but is constantly threatened and terrorized by the brothers. When the brothers stalk Clara, Amos makes a gutsy attempt to save her. This book contains some rough parts, poor adult role models, and depressing family life/values, but strong main characters.

Stanley, Diane. *A Time Apart*. Morrow Junior Books, 1999.

Ginny's mother is ill with cancer and undergoing treatments, so she sends Ginny to England to live with her dad who is a professor living in a yearlong experimental Iron Age village. Thirteen-year-old Ginny is upset about leaving her friends in Houston, Texas, to live with strangers and her dad—whom she hasn't seen in a year—in this strange setting. Yet she actually finds herself enjoying it; she is a good cook and makes friends with a small child, an older teenager, and adult members of the group. When she runs away to go home to her mother, her dad comes after her and goes too. She realizes her mother needs time to work through her treatments, so Ginny returns with her father to England and finishes out the time. All through the story you get a really clear picture of what life is thought to have been like in an Iron Age village.

Annotated Professional Journal Articles

Hewitt, Margaret, and Ande Dervaes. "Is Our Continued Efferent Stance Toward Reading in Middle and High Schools Discouraging Students' Love of Reading?" *The Florida Reading Quarterly* (December 1999): 20-23.

Assignments are still given for which the student's grade depends on how well the student's response to the reading reflects the teacher's idea of what was intended by the author. The student's understanding or feelings become insignificant. Our goal should be that readers can comprehend the story through the personal meanings they create while reading. When students read a novel for class, they know they must take an efferent stance when reading because they are going to be asked for the main idea, theme, character flaws, foreshadowing, and author's intent. The article provides a variety of activities that support an aesthetic stance when reading novels for the classroom.

Towle, Wendy. "The Art of the Reading Workshop," *Educational Leadership* (September 2000): 38-41.

Reading workshop is an approach to reading instruction that provides a framework for teachers to meet the needs of all readers. It allows the teacher to provide one-on-one instructional time with each student every week. Teachers assume that because all of the students can read chapter books, all students should read the same book and receive whole class instruction. But this does not allow for each student's strengths and needs. In reading workshop students spend their time reading and writing to construct meaning. There are five components: teacher sharing time, focus lessons, state of class conference, self-selected reading and responding time, and student sharing time. The article gives practical ideas for conducting reading workshop, including detailed directions for each of the five components, information on conducting effective individual student conferences, and guidelines for assessment and record keeping.

Wilson, Nance. "Easing Students into Reader Response," *The Florida Reading Quarterly* (March 1999): 20-23.

The author claims that because her students had not been asked to write responses before, the results were dismal. Students are used to giving the right answer and to writing what they think the teacher wants to hear. So when they were simply asked to respond to their reading, they were unsure what was expected. This teacher established a step-by-step guide in which she first asked for a brief summary of the reading and then provided the students with a list of questions or unfinished statements asking for personal involvement with the story. The third part involved the story's literary elements and asked the students to respond to the writer's style. This section again included general questions about literary elements. The students then made their personal connections to the story. The last part asked for predictions and questions, and again some general questions and unfinished statements were provided to help the student become personally involved with the story. This article provides an excellent framework for thoughtful reader responses.

Annotated Professional Books

Allen, Janet, and Kyle Gonzalez. *There's Room for Me Here: Literacy Workshop in the Middle School.* Stenhouse Publishers, 1998.

   This book is about the literacy classroom of a middle school teacher who helps struggling readers. It provides information on establishing a literacy workshop; selecting and using effective resources; implementing appropriate record keeping; helping students establish goals; using read alouds, shared, guided, and independent reading; and helping students become effective content area readers. The book includes useful forms and extensive bibliographies.

Atwell, Nancie. *In the Middle: New Understandings about Writing, Reading, and Learning.* Heinemann, 1998.

   Certainly this is the most important book for any middle level teacher to have. The chapters include how to teach reading and writing, making the best of adolescence, mini-lessons, responses, and evaluating. The book is filled with samples of student work and appendixes rich with charts, surveys, checklists, records, and other useful reproducibles.

Beers, Kylene, and Barbara Samuels, eds. *Into Focus: Understanding and Creating Middle School Readers.* Christopher-Gordon, 1998.

   There are 22 essays in this volume written by 27 authors on a wide variety of topics of interest to those working with middle school students. The topics include understanding middle school students, choosing not to read, gifted middle school readers, struggling readers, reader response theory, thematic units and readers workshop, literature discussions, literature circles, journals, content area reading, authentic reading assessment, short stories, novels, and reading on the Internet.

Blass, Rosanne, and Nancy Allen. *Responding to Literature: Activities for Grades 6, 7, 8.* Teacher Ideas Press, 1991.

   This book provides a variety of activities for responding to literature using games, music, dance, drama, writing, art, focused listening, oral expression, discovery learning, and group problem solving. There is also an extensive bibliography of appropriate titles.

Booth, David, ed. *Literacy Techniques for Building Successful Readers and Writers.* Pembroke, 1996.

   This is a comprehensive handbook for teaching reading and writing—a collection of strategies and an overview of 100 major approaches to encourage literacy. Each approach includes a brief discussion of the issues and then focuses on ready-to-use ideas for the classroom. Topics include assessment, literature circles, thematic units, journals, vocabulary, peer tutors, mini-lessons, and much more.

Bullock, Richard, ed. *Why Workshop? Changing Course in 7-12 English*. Stenhouse Publishers, 1998.

This book has nine essays written by experienced teachers. There is information on using writing and reading workshops as the primary organization method for language arts classrooms. One essay deals with responses to literature and offers useful suggestions. The book includes a very complete workshop course plan.

Calkins, Lucy. *The Art of Teaching Reading*. Addison-Wesley Longman, 2000.

All areas of reading are included here from reading aloud, assessment, phonics, and word study to a whole section on reading workshop and responses, book clubs, and writing about reading. The book also discusses story elements, strategies, nonfiction, and reading projects. There are appendixes with lists of children's books, magazines for kids, and examples of leveled reading books.

Gambrell, Linda, and Janice Almasi, eds. *Lively Discussions! Fostering Engaged Reading*. International Reading Association, 1996.

Twenty-three different authors share their thoughts on topics such as using multiple texts, student-led discussions, literature in a multicultural classroom, types of informational texts, creating a response-centered curriculum, and story retelling and other comprehension strategies.

Hetzel, June. *Responding to Literature: Activities to Use with Any Literature Selection*. Creative Teaching Press, 1993.

Generic reproducible activities are provided to enhance reading comprehension skills for any novel. Questions and activities that encourage higher level thinking skills, interaction with literature on a personal level, and creative writing are also included.

Jackson, Norma, with Paula Pillow. *The Reading-Writing Workshop: Getting Started*. Scholastic Professional Books, 1992.

All the necessary details for setting up a reading/writing workshop are covered in this book. It includes information on what the workshop is, how it works, and how students and teachers keep track of work—and there are reproducible forms for making management easier. There is a chapter on organizing the classroom and suggestions for literature focus and skill lessons, projects, and themes. There is also an extensive bibliography of professional and children's books.

Langer, Judith. *Envisioning Literature: Literary Understanding and Literature Instruction*. Teachers College Press, 1995.

Interacting with texts, literary discussions, strategies for teaching, literature for students the system has failed, literary concepts and vocabulary, and literature across the curriculum are some of the topics discussed in this book about literature for middle and high school students.

Muschla, G. *Reading Workshop Survival Kit.* Center for Applied Research in Education, 1997.

Here is everything you need to set up and teach an effective reading workshop where reading is the priority. Part one furnishes guidelines and tools for creating and managing a reading workshop in the classroom. It also offers background information on the process. Part two provides ready-to-use mini-lessons with worksheets that focus on reading and related topics, story elements, and a variety of specific reading skills.

Parsons, Les. *Response Journals.* Heinemann, 1990.

This is a rather old publication date, but the information remains timely. The book contains ideas and information about the importance of response journals in literature classes. There are chapters on student-teacher conferences, small group discussions, evaluating response journals, and a checklist for planning the classroom environment.

Rosenblatt, Louise. *The Reader, The Text, The Poem: The Transactional Theory of the Literary Work.* Southern Illinois University Press, 1978.

This is Rosenblatt's premier work on the transactional theory of reading. A text is simply words, paper, and ink until the reader makes it a literacy work. The reader reacts differently in efferent and aesthetic reading. The reading of any work is an individual and unique experience involving the mind and emotions of each reader.

Routman, Regie. *Conversations: Strategies for Teaching, Learning, and Evaluating.* Heinemann, 2000.

Fifteen chapters on literacy provide information about the teacher as a professional; the literacy program; teaching children to read; encouraging children to discuss their reading, writing, journals, spelling and word study; reading nonfiction; effective questioning; collaboration; and evaluation. The book also contains an extensive section of blue pages that contain resources for teachers.

Soter, Anna. *Young Adult Literature and the New Library Theories: Developing Critical Readers in the Middle School.* Teachers College Press, 2000.

The first chapter discusses alternative approaches to teaching young adult fiction. The author looks seriously at using young adult literature in the classroom and at ways of "teaching" it by recognizing that the ways students connect with a story and make meaning from it are often overlooked in literature classes. The remaining chapters focus on young adult titles, including *The Island, Homecoming, My Brother Sam Is Dead, Where the Lilies Bloom, The True Confessions of Charlotte Doyle, Somewhere in the Darkness,* and *Requiem.* It concludes with a chapter on literature responses.

Spencer, P. *What Do Young Adults Read Next? A Reader's Guide to Fiction for Young Adults.* Gale Research, 1994.

This is a reader's advisory tool designed to match young adults with books that reflect their interests and concerns. It guides both reluctant and avid readers to seek new titles and authors for further reading. Each entry provides information on the author and the title and even recommends a list of alternate selections. The introductory essay gives a complete history of young adult literature and recent trends in the field. Ten indexes help locate specific titles or titles by geographic locales, special subjects or characters, or by age level.

Spencer, P. *What Do Young Adults Read Next? Volume Two: A Reader's Guide to Fiction for Young Adults.* Gale Research, 1997.

A follow-up to volume one, this is a reader's advisory tool with much the same format as the first one, but it focuses more on recent titles and authors in the field of young adult literature.

Wilhelm, Jeffrey. *You've Gotta BE the Book: Teaching Engaged and Reflective Reading with Adolescents.* Teachers College Press, 1995.

Many case studies are noted in this book. It has chapters about reading-centered classrooms, engaged student readers, reading response, using drama to extend reading, visualization, and expanding concepts of reading, response, and literature. The Ten Dimensions of Reader Response are discussed.

Wollman-Bonilla, Julie. *Response Journals.* Scholastic Professional Books, 1992.

The use of response journals, how to get started, replying to students' responses, dealing with problems, and a variety of activities related to response journals are all included. This volume includes a bibliography and suggested books and articles for further reading.

Web Sites

Ask the Author
    http://www.ipl.org/youth/AskAuthor/AskAuthor.html

Authors
    http://web.nwe.ufl.edu/~jbrown/chauth.html

Booklist Magazine
    http://www.ala.org/booklist/index.html

Bookwire
    http://www.bookwire.com

Children and Young Adult Literature and Culture Links
    http://ebbs.english.vt.edu/chla/morelinks.html

Children's and Young Adults' Authors and Illustrators
    http://falcon.jmu.edu/~ramseyil/biochildhome.htm

The Children's Literature Web Guide
    http://www.acs.ucalgary/~dkbrown/

Cooperative Children's Book Center
    http://www.soemadison.wisc.edu/ccbc/

Harry Potter Web Quest
    http://www.connectingstudents.com/lessonplans/potter/

International Reading Association
    http://www.ira.org

Invite an Author
    http://www.snowcrest.net/kidpower/authors.html

Kids Web Literature
    http://www.kidsvista.com/Arts/literature.html

KitLit Children's Literature Home Page
    http://mgfx.com/kidlit/

Lists of Recommended Books
    http://www.eduplace.com/rdg/links/rdg_16.html

NCTE Teaching Ideas—Reading
    http://www.ncte.org/teach/read.html

The Official Site—Goosebumps
    http://www.scholastic.com/goosebumps/index.htm

The Read In!
    http://www.readin.org/

Reading Rants
    http://tln.lib.mi.us/~amutch/jen/index.html

Scholastic Books
    http://www.scholastic.com

School Library Journal Online
    http://www.schoollibraryjournal.com

World of Reading
    http://www.worldreading.org/

Young Adult Library Services Association
    http://www.ala.org/yalsa/

Young Adult Literature
    http://yahelp.suffolk.lib.ny.us/yalit.html

6

Literature Circles

Daniels (1994) states that literature circles are a reading strategy that combine the principles of cooperative learning, independent reading, and group discussion. They are important in helping students become lifelong readers. Literature circles promote reading and foster literary discussion.

The power of collaborative grouping is well documented. In fact, collaborative learning has been defined as a key ingredient of "best educational practice." It is open-ended and student centered, and the limited size of the groups compels each member to be an active participant and a responsible group member.

Research also shows that independent reading is the single factor most strongly associated with reading achievement. Students who choose books for themselves and read on their own become the strongest readers.

Daniels (1994) also points out that literature circles manifest most or all of these key features:

- Students choose their own reading materials.

- Small temporary groups are formed based on book choice.

- Different groups read different books.

- Groups meet on a regular schedule to discuss their reading.

- Students take notes to guide them in their reading and discussion.

- Discussion topics come from the students.

- Group meetings aim to be open, natural conversations about books so personal connections, digressions, and open-ended questions are welcome.

- In newly formed groups students play a rotating assortment of task roles.

- The teacher serves as a facilitator, not a group member or instructor.

- Evaluation is by teacher observation and student self/group evaluation.

- When books are finished readers share with their classmates, then new groups are formed around new reading choices.

Rosenblatt (1978) states that reading is a transaction; it is a two-way process between the reader and the text at a special time and with certain circumstances. What each reader brings to the reading can effect the connection or outcome.

In literature circles, discussions follow individual responses or reactions to the reading. The discussions are not based on answering teacher-directed questions, according to Langer (1995).

Calkins (2000) thinks that teachers feel guilty if their students are spending a class period free reading. Teachers somehow feel they are not teaching if they allow students to make their own choices and find their own meaning in what they read.

Daniels (1994) also feels that because of the focus on testing, teachers do not feel comfortable with the kinds of assessment associated with literature circles. The tools of kidwatching, narrative observational logs, checklists, student conferences, and group interviews are the evaluation equipment. In literature circles teachers require that students take responsibility for their own book selections, topic choices, role sheets, reading assignments, record keeping, and self and group evaluations.

Noe and Johnson (1999) claim that when readers discuss insights, raise questions, cite related experiences, and wonder about or puzzle over situations prompted by what they read, literature takes on a new life. Interpretation is dynamic. But it is limited when we read alone. When we provide our students with a place to discuss their own interpretation and listen to other readers add their interpretation, a book becomes even more meaningful. Rather than passively waiting for others to impose questions and assign worksheets, students involved in discussion raise their own questions and consider their own experiences.

Group discussions are an important element of literature circles. In order to foster discussion, quality open-ended questions are necessary. The following lists are excellent sources of good questions to promote energetic and thoughtful discussions.

- What incident, problem, conflict, or situation does the author use to get the story started?

- What does the author do to create suspense, to make you want to read on to find out what happens?

- Think of a different ending to the story. How would the rest of the story have to be changed to fit the new ending?

- Did the story end the way you expected it to?

- Are any characters changed during the story? If they are, how are they different? What changed them? Did it seem believable?

- Does the story as a whole create a certain mood or feeling? What is the mood? How is it created?

- Did you have strong feelings as you read the story? What did the author do to make you feel strongly?

- Is this story like any other story you have read or watched?

—Sloan, G. *The Child as Critic.* Teachers College Press, 1984.

◂◂ What idea or ideas does this story make you think about? How does the author get you to think about this?

◂◂ Do any particular feelings come across in this story? Does the story actually make you feel in a certain way or does it make you think about what it's like to feel that way? How does the author do this?

◂◂ Is there one character that you know more about than any of the others? What words would you use to describe the main character's feelings in this book?

◂◂ Is there anything that seems to make this particular author's work unique? If so, what?

◂◂ If you are reading this book in more than one sitting, are there natural points at which to break off your reading? If so, what are these?

◂◂ Were there any clues that the author built into the story that helped you to anticipate the outcome? Did you think these clues were important when you read them?

◂◂ What questions would you ask if the author were here? Which would be the most important question? How might the author answer it?

—Vandergrift, K. *Child and Story*. Neal-Schuman, 1980.

Professional Discussion Questions

1. What characteristics do you look for when you select a book for literature circles?

2. What are ways to manage literature circles?

3. What are ways to assess literature circles?

4. Is it necessary for students to have roles assigned?

5. When does a teacher step into a discussion?

6. How often can you include literature circles in your reading program?

7. Is it ever appropriate for teachers to select the students for the literature circles?

8. How can librarians or other teachers promote literature circles among their colleagues?

Practical Application

Sample Literature Circles with Annotated Young Adult Literature

Decisions and Choices

Anderson, Laurie Halse. *Speak*. Farrar Straus and Giroux, 1999.

Melinda starts ninth grade as an outcast. She called the police during a summer party and now she has no friends; she doesn't speak to anyone and her grades continue to drop. She finally faces her demon and her friends begin to return. The story is told in a very current style.

Holt, Kimberly Willis. *My Louisiana Sky*. Henry Holt and Company, 1998.

"Your momma may have a simple mind, tiger; but her love is simple too. It flows from her like a quick, easy river."

Tiger isn't sure when she first became aware of other people's reaction to her mother and father. Both of her parents are mentally deficient. However, Tiger's granny is very strong and sensible and she keeps the family together. What will happen when Granny dies? Will Tiger get her wish and leave the small Louisiana town and live with Aunt Dorie Kay? Through it all, Tiger will grow up a little faster and wiser.

Myers, Walter Dean. *Monster*. HarperCollins Children's Book Group, 1999.

Steven Harmon, 16, is on trial for murder. He is witnessing and scripting his own trial as if he were producing a movie. Throughout this unusual format one has a sense of how and why this murder was committed and the pressures these young men endure both in and out of prison. At one point Steve asks, "You think we're going to win?" His attorney responds, "It probably depends on what you mean by 'win'." There are no winners in this thought-provoking novel.

Randle, Kristen D. *Breaking Rank*. Morrow Junior Books, 1999.

Baby has spent most of his life as a member of a group called the Clan. They wear black and are generally feared and scorned by classmates and neighbors. He goes against the group and takes honor classes in high school and is assigned a peer tutor—a pretty, well-liked girl named Casey. Casey helps Baby get into the mainstream at school, but this threatens the Clan and the Cribs, the popular kids who wear letter jackets. Soon, the inevitable happens and the choices have to be made.

Tarbox, Katherine. *Katie.Com*. Dutton, 2000.

This is the true story of Katie Tarbox, age 13. Katie is a nationally ranked swimmer from a well-to-do family. Katie's mom worked long hours and Katie was left alone unsupervised. She entered a chat room in 1995 and met Mark. They sent e-mails and talked on the telephone for over six months. Katie was participating in a swim meet in Texas, and Mark was going to fly from California to meet her. Naive Katie went up to his room, and shortly thereafter Katie's mom, her coaches, and security were at the door. This was only the beginning of changes for Katie. She was ostracized at home, swimming, and school. Eventually she learned that Mark was really Frank, age 41, an Internet pedophile, who plea-bargained and was incarcerated for 18 months. During this whole painful experience Katie's moods went from guilt, fear, and shame until finally she no longer felt like a victim.

▣ **Discussion Questions:**

1. Compare and contrast the decisions and choices the protagonists made and the consequences of their actions.

2. Are you satisfied with the ending?

3. Are these books realistic?

Fantasy

Matas, Carol, and Perry Nodelman. *Of Two Minds.* Simon & Schuster Books for Young Readers, 1995.

Princess Lenore of Gepeth is a headstrong, imaginative young woman who is betrothed to Prince Coren of Andilla. Each of them possesses powers that the other one does not have. Coren is able to enter another person's mind and read thoughts. Lenore is able to create other situations and fantasies and have them come true. In the midst of their wedding, Lenore sees her chance to escape, and she does—only Coren flees with her. They find themselves in a world controlled by a glamorous tyrant named Hevak who shares the same powers as Lenore. How the two royals escape leads to an ending with a twist.

Napoli, Donna Jo. *Zel.* Dutton Children's Books, 1996.

This is the young adult story of the fairy tale "Rapunzel," told in alternating chapters from the point of view of Zel, Mother, and Konrad, the young noble. Zel is an innocent 13-year-old girl who is locked in a tower by her mother. Mother was a childless woman who gave up her soul to acquire Zel. Zel's real name is Rapunzel, a type of lettuce. Her birth mother craved Rapunzel lettuce so much that Mother bewitched her husband into trading the lettuce for the newborn baby.

Mother happily raised Zel but could not share her—thus the tower. Konrad, after a brief earlier encounter with Zel, searches for two years to find her. Ultimately, he succeeds, but not before Mother blinds Konrad and has Zel carried off by the trees. After another two years, Konrad finds Zel. Zel's tears run into Konrad's eyes and he sees. They are happy at long last.

Rowling, J. K. *Harry Potter and the Prisoner of Azkaban.* Scholastic Incorporated, 2000.

Harry is in his third year at Hogwarts. The escaped prisoner is Sirius Black, and it is rumored that he is after Harry. This adventure has a griffin and lots of great adventures and magical tricks.

Shusterman, Neal. *Downsiders: A Novel.* Simon & Schuster Books for Young Readers, 1999.

Beneath New York City lies a strange and secret world called Downside. The people who live there know it is forbidden to go Topside, but 14-year-old Talon is curious about what goes on above ground. He searches for medicine for his sister Pidge, who has flulike symptoms. Lindsay, also 14, has just been dumped in New York City to live with her father and stepbrother by her newly divorced, career-student mother. She makes friends with Talon, supplies him with some leftover antibiotics, and eventually he takes her for a forbidden visit to Downside. Lindsay's dad is a city engineer working on an underground aqueduct. During his excavating he discovers Downside, and the future of Downside and its inhabitants is in question.

Sleator, William. *Rewind.* Dutton Children's Books, 1999.

Peter is killed in a car accident and then hears a voice and sees the bright light. The offer is to try it again to see if he can change the events that lead up to his death. He goes back and tries, only to be killed a second and a third time. There is an interesting relationship between Peter, who is adopted, and his parents, who are expecting their first natural child. There are also complicated relationships between Peter and a class bully, an art teacher, and a female classmate. This is a very different story.

Zindel, Paul. *Rats.* Hyperion Books for Children, 1999.

Mutant rats living in the Staten Island landfill do not like it when the dump is paved over. They leave and try to get to New York City. Sarah and Michael and their pet rat, Surfer, try to figure out what is happening and why. Surfer ends up siding with the rats. The book has lots of descriptive details of gory killings. Sarah and Michael race all over the area in boats, and never mind the adults taking care of them. But in the end, they save the day.

▣ **Discussion Questions:**

1. What is it about fantasy that makes this genre so popular?
2. Would you like to live in the world as it is portrayed in the book?
3. What makes this book a fantasy?

Bibliography

Auch, Mary Jane. *Journey to Nowhere.* Bantam Doubleday Dell Books for Young Readers, 1997.

Avi. *Something Upstairs.* Avon Books, 1988.

———. *The True Confessions of Charlotte Doyle.* Avon Books, 1990.

———. *Poppy.* Avon Books, 1995.

Ayres, Katherine. *Family Tree.* Bantam Doubleday Dell Books for Young Readers, 1996.

Babbitt, Natalie. *Tuck Everlasting.* Farrar, Straus and Giroux, 1975.

Ballard, Robert D. *Exploring the Titanic.* A Scholastic/Madison Press Book, 1988.

Bauer, Joan. *Rules of the Road.* G. P. Putnam's Sons, 1988.

———. *Sticks.* Bantam Doubleday Dell Books for Young Readers, 1996.

Beattie, Owen, and John Geiger. *Buried in Ice.* A Scholastic/Madison Press Book, 1992.

Birdseye, Tom. *Tarantula Shoes*. Puffin Books, 1995.

Blackwood, Gary. *The Shakespeare Stealer*. Dutton Children's Books, 1998.

Bledsoe, Lucy Jane. *Tracks in the Snow*. Holiday House, 1997.

Bloor, Edward. *Tangerine*. Scholastic Incorporated, 1997.

Boyd, Candy Dawson. *Chevrolet Saturdays*. Puffin Books, 1993.

Brink, Carol Ryrie. *Caddie Woodlawn*. Scholastic Incorporated, 1935.

Bruchac, Joseph. *Eagle Song*. Puffin Books, 1997.

Bunting, Eve. *The In-Between Days*. HarperTrophy, 1994.

———. *Nasty, Stinky Sneakers*. HarperTrophy, 1994.

Burnett, Frances Hodgson. *The Secret Garden*. J. B. Lippincott Company, 1911.

Burnford, Sheila. *The Incredible Journey*. Bantam Books, 1960.

Clements, Andrew. *Frindle*. Aladdin Paperbacks, 1996.

Collier, James Lincoln. *My Brother Sam Is Dead*. Scholastic Incorporated, 1974.

Cooper, Susan. *The Boggart*. Aladdin Paperbacks, 1993.

Cooney, Caroline B. *Flight #116 Is Down*. Scholastic Incorporated, 1992.

Coville, Bruce. *Into the Land of the Unicorns*. Scholastic Incorporated, 1994.

Creech, Sharon. *Pleasing the Ghost*. HarperTrophy, 1996.

Cullen, Lynn. *The Three Lives of Harris Harper*. Avon Books, 1996.

Curtis, Christopher Paul. *The Watsons Go to Birmingham—1963*. Scholastic Incorporated, 1995.

Cushman, Karen. *Catherine Called Birdy*. HarperTrophy, 1994.

DeFelice, Cynthia. *The Light on Hogback Hill*. Avon Books, 1993.

———. *The Apprenticeship of Lucas Whitaker*. Avon Books, 1996.

Dorris, Michael. *Sees Behind Trees*. Hyperion Paperbacks for Children, 1996.

du Bois, William Pene. *The Twenty-One Balloons*. Puffin Books, 1947.

Duffey, Betsy. *Coaster*. Puffin Books, 1994.

———. *Utterly Yours, Booker Jones*. Puffin Books, 1995.

Eckert, Allan W. *Incident at Hawk's Hill*. Bantam Books, 1971.

Farmer, Nancy. *The Ear, the Eye and the Arm*. Puffin Books, 1994.

Fletcher, Ralph. *Shadow Spinner*. Atheneum Books for Young Readers, 1988.

———. *Fig Pudding*. Bantam Doubleday Dell Books for Young Readers, 1995.

Franklin, Kristine L. *Lone Wolf.* Candlewick Press, 1997.

Gantos, Jack. *Joey Pigza Swallowed the Key.* Farrar Straus and Giroux, 1988.

Garland, Sherry. *Cabin 102.* Harcourt Brace and Company, 1995.

George, Jean Craighead. *There's an Owl in the Shower.* HarperTrophy, 1995.

Giff, Patricia Reilly. *Lily's Crossing.* Bantam Doubleday Dell Books for Young Readers, 1997.

Gordon, Sheila. *Waiting for the Rain.* Bantam Books, 1987.

Griffin, Peni R. *The Treasure Bird.* Puffin Books, 1994.

Gutman, Dan. *Honus & Me.* Avon Books, 1997.

Haddix, Margaret Peterson. *Running Out of Time.* Aladdin Paperbacks, 1995.

———. *Among the Hidden.* Simon & Schuster Books for Young Readers, 1998.

Hahn, Mary Downing. *Time for Andrew: A Ghost Story.* Avon Books, 1994.

Henkes, Kevin. *Sun & Spoon.* Puffin Books, 1997.

Hermes, Patricia. *Nothing But Trouble, Trouble, Trouble.* Scholastic Incorporated, 1994.

Hobbs, Will. *Far North.* Avon Books, 1996.

Karr, Kathleen. *The Great Turkey Walk.* Farrar Straus and Giroux, 1988.

Kehret, Peg. *The Volcano Disaster.* A Minstrel Book, 1998.

Lawrence, Iain. *The Wreckers.* Delacorte Press, 1998.

Levine, Gail Carson. *Ella Enchanted.* Scholastic Incorporated, 1997.

Lobel, Anita. *No Pretty Pictures: A Child of War.* Greenwillow Books, 1998.

Mackel, Kathy. *A Season of Comebacks.* The Putnam & Grosset Group, 1997.

Matas, Carol. *Of Two Minds.* Scholastic Incorporated. 1995.

———. *Greater Than Angels.* Aladdin Paperbacks, 1998.

McKissack, Patricia C. *Run Away Home.* Scholastic Incorporated, 1997.

Mikelson, Ben. *Sparrow Hawk Red.* Hyperion Paperbacks for Children, 1993.

———. *Stranded.* Hyperion Paperbacks for Children, 1995.

———. *Countdown.* Hyperion Paperbacks for Children, 1996

Mills, Claudia. *Losers, Inc.* Scholastic Incorporated, 1997.

Montgomery, Lucy Maud. *Anne of Green Gables.* Barnes & Noble Books, 1994.

Myers, Walter Dean. *Monster.* HarperCollins, 1999.

Namoli, Donna Jo. *Stones in the Water.* Scholastic Incorporated, 1997.

Naylor, Phyllis Reynolds. *Shiloh Season.* Aladdin Paperbacks, 1996.

Nelson, Vaundra Micheaux. *Possibles.* The Putnam & Grosset Group, 1995.

Nixon, Joan Lowry. *Shadowmaker.* Bantam Doubleday Dell Books for Young Readers, 1994.

———. *Search for the Shadowman.* Bantam Doubleday Dell Books for Young Readers, 1996.

———. *Circle of Love.* Bantam Doubleday Dell Books for Young Readers, 1997.

O'Brien, Robert C. *Mrs. Frisby and the Rats of NIMH.* Aladdin Paperbacks, 1971.

O'Grady, Captain Scott. *Basher Five-Two.* Puffin Books, 1996.

Paterson, Katherine. *Lyddie.* Puffin Books, 1991.

———. *Jip: His Story.* Puffin Books, 1996.

Paulsen, Gary. *The River.* Bantam Doubleday Dell Publishing Group, 1991.

———. *Mr. Tucket.* Bantam Doubleday Dell Books for Young Readers, 1994.

———. *Brian's Winter.* Bantam Doubleday Dell Books for Young Readers, 1996.

Peck, Richard. *Lost in Cyberspace.* Puffin Books, 1995.

Petersen, P. J. *The Sub.* Puffin Books, 1993.

Ransom, Candice F. *Fire in the Sky.* Carolrhoda Books, Incorporated, 1997.

Raskin, Ellen. *The Westing Game.* Puffin Books, 1978.

Reeder, Carolyn. *Shades of Gray.* Avon Books, 1989.

Reiss, Johanna. *The Upstairs Room.* Bantam Books, 1972.

Reuter, Bjarne. *The Boys from St. Petri.* Puffin Books, 1991.

Roberts, Willo Davis. *Don't Hurt Laurie.* Aladdin Paperbacks, 1977.

———. *The Kidnappers: A Mystery.* Aladdin Paperbacks, 1998.

Robertson, Barbara. *The Best School Year Ever.* HarperTrophy, 1994.

Ryan, Pam Muñoz. *Riding Freedom.* Scholastic Incorporated, 1998.

Ryden, Hope. *Wild Horse Summer.* Bantam Doubleday Dell Books for Young Readers, 1997.

Sachar, Louis. *Holes.* Farrar Straus and Giroux, 1998.

Skurzynski, Gloria. *Virtual War.* Aladdin Paperbacks, 1997.

Sleator, William. *Others See Us.* Puffin Books, 1993.

Smith, Roland. *Jaguar.* Hyperion Paperbacks for Children, 1997.

Speare, Elizabeth George. *The Witch of Blackbird Pond.* Laurel-Leaf Books, 1958.

Spinelli, Jerry. *Crash.* Alfred A. Knopf, 1996.

Stolz, Mary. *Stealing Home.* HarperTrophy, 1992.

Tanaka, Shelley. *The Buried City of Pompeii.* A Hyperion/Madison Press Book, 1997.

Taylor, Theodore. *Timothy of the Cay.* Avon Books, 1993.

———. *The Bomb.* Avon Books, 1995.

Wallace, Bill. *True Friends.* A Minstrel Book, 1994.

Wardlaw, Lee. *101 Ways to Bug Your Parents.* Bantam Doubleday Dell Books for Young Readers, 1996.

Westall, Robert. *Gulf.* Scholastic Incorporated, 1992.

Williams, Laura E. *Behind the Bedroom Wall.* Scholastic Incorporated, 1996.

Wisler, G. Clifton. *Thunder on the Tennessee.* Puffin Books, 1983.

———. *Red Cap.* Puffin Books, 1991.

———. *Mr. Lincoln's Drummer.* Scholastic Incorporated, 1995.

———. *Caleb's Choice.* Puffin Books, 1996.

Wood, June Rae. *When Pigs Fly.* G. P. Putnam's Sons, 1995.

Woodruff, Elvira. *Ghosts Don't Get Goosebumps.* Bantam Doubleday Dell Books for Young Readers, 1993.

———. *The Secret Funeral of Slim Jim the Snake.* Bantam Doubleday Dell Books for Young Readers, 1993.

Yep, Laurence. *Dragon's Gate.* HarperCollins, 1993.

———. *The Case of the Goblin Pearls.* HarperTrophy, 1997.

Yolen, Jane. *The Devil's Arithmetic.* Puffin Books, 1988.

Annotated Professional Journal Articles

Burns, B. "Changing the Classroom Climate with Literature Circles," *Journal of Adolescent & Adult Literacy* (October 1998): 124-28.

Literature circles change the classroom climate to be more supportive for students to take greater academic risks. Literature circles incorporate student choice, groups of mixed ability, student management of small interactive groups, and substantial time to read during the school day. Burns's literature circles offer students a limited selection of books around a central theme. Burns booktalks all titles, lets the students make their selections, and then she creates the groups. The students decide within their group how they will read the book—by pages or chapters—and how they will complete their reading within the two-week time limit. The students are assigned roles within the groups. All students had very positive comments about having choice and time in class for reading.

Edinger, Monica. "How to Lead Better Book Talks," *Instructor* (May/June 1995): 60-64.

The teacher must set up an accepting and open environment to encourage all children to express their ideas. This author likes to lead a discussion of 10 to 12 students, and she uses the classics and student-choice books in their reading program. The discussions focus on the character, writing style, illustrations, and themes. "Reading, talking, writing, and responding to good literature are at the heart of my language arts program."

Giorgis, Cyndi, and Kimberly J. Hartman. "Using Picture Books to Support Middle School Curricula," *Middle School Journal* (March 2000): 34-41.

"It is important that 'picture book' is a descriptive term related to format. A picture book generally contains 32 pages with pictures appearing on every page or double-page spread." The authors discuss several picture books that could be used in the various disciplines: reading and language arts, social studies, science, math, and fine arts.

Hurst, Carol Otis. "Picture Books in the Middle School," *Teaching K-8* (November/December 1997): 50-51.

The author, Carol Hurst, discusses many suitable picture books for the middle school curricula. She also includes the URL addresses of her children's literature site and one for Onyx Press, which offers suggestions for using 43 award-winning picture books: http://carolhurst.com and http://www.oryxpress.com/books.pbl.htm.

Hurst, Carol Otis. "Meaningful Picture Books," *Teaching K-8* (May 2000): 92-99.

In the column "In the Library," Carol Otis Hurst uses picture books to gain a different perspective on history, science, math, and larger issues as well. She uses old favorites such as Dr. Seuss's *The 500 Hats of Bartholomew* and *Why Mosquitoes Buzz in People's Ears* as well as humorous books and alphabet books. All could be used in unique ways to get across the point that one can look at something in more than one way.

Katz, C., S. Kuby, and J. Hobgood. "Trapped in a Month of Mondays," *Journal of Adolescent & Adult Literacy* (October 1997): 152-55.

This is a short story about a teacher who dreams about her students and the fact that they seem unmotivated and listless. A vampire visits the classroom bringing interesting statistics about the usefulness of literature circles. Her students do listen to her booktalks and make selections as a direct result, and they are reading more. The teacher "wakes up" to her students returning to the classroom and the normal class setting as she assigns sustained silent reading.

Scott, Jill. "Literature Circles in the Middle School Classroom: Developing Reading, Responding, and Responsibility," *Middle School Journal* (November 1994): 37-41.

A seventh grade teacher discusses how she uses literature circles to link reading, writing, and classroom talk in an authentic manner and to create a community of learners. Scott says that she was using reading workshop exclusively in her class but realized that something was missing. That something was student talk about literature. Using literature circles for part of the time helped students converse about literature, share personal responses to reading, use their social nature to invite reading and thinking, and promote acceptance of others as literature circles do not group by ability. The article describes exactly how Scott set up very effective literature circles with her classes.

Annotated Professional Books

Ammon, Bette D., and Gale W. Sherman. *Worth a Thousand Words: An Annotated Guide to Picture Books for Older Readers*. Libraries Unlimited, 1996.

"Traditionally a picture book is defined as a story told using two media, a blending of verbal and visual art where the pictures and the text work independently to tell a story." The 645 books are arranged alphabetically by author, editor, or title if no credit is given. Each title includes complete publishing information, an annotation, and extensive listing of themes, subjects, and genres. Ideas on how the book could be used in the curriculum follow each entry. Indexes include author/illustrator, subject, and title.

Beers, Kylene, and Barbara Samuels, eds. *Into Focus: Understanding and Creating Middle School Readers.* Christopher-Gordon, 1998.

There are 22 essays in this volume written by 27 authors on a wide variety of topics of interest to those working with middle school students. The topics include understanding middle school students, choosing not to read, gifted middle school readers, struggling readers, reader response theory, thematic units and readers workshop, literature discussions, literature circles, journals, content area reading, authentic reading assessment, short stories, novels, and reading on the Internet.

Benedict, Susan, and Lenore Carlisle, eds. *Beyond Words: Picture Books for Older Readers and Writers.* Heinemann, 1992.

Fifteen authors share how they have used picture books effectively with older readers in 14 practical essays. Picture books help to introduce a topic, spark creativity, prompt discussions and sharing, and set a pattern for older kids to create picture books for younger students on topics that they are studying.

Booth, David, ed. *Literacy Techniques for Building Successful Readers and Writers.* Pembroke, 1996.

This is a comprehensive handbook for teaching reading and writing—a collection of strategies and an overview of 100 major approaches to encourage literacy. Each approach includes a brief discussion of the issues and then focuses on ready-to-use ideas for the classroom. Topics include assessment, literature circles, thematic units, journals, vocabulary, peer tutors, mini-lessons, and much more.

Calkins, Lucy. *The Art of Teaching Reading*. Addison-Wesley Longman, 2001.

Calkin's latest book provides teachers with all they need to instill the love of reading and assure reading success for all their students. It includes insights and information on independent reading, guided reading, booktalks, word study, reading aloud, reading workshop, book clubs, and many other areas. This is a companion volume to Calkin's book, *The Art of Writing*.

Daniels, Harvey. *Literature Circles: Voice and Choice in the Student-Centered Classroom.* Stenhouse Publishers, 1994.

Included here is everything you need to know about literature circles—getting started, managing groups, materials, record keeping, evaluating and grading, problems, questions and variations—for all levels from primary grades through college.

Langer, Judith. *Envisioning Literature: Literacy Understanding and Literature Instruction.* Teachers College Press 1995.

Interacting with texts, literacy discussions, strategies for teaching, literature for students the system has failed, literacy concepts and vocabulary, and literature across the curriculum are some of the topics discussed in this book about literature for middle and high school students.

McElmeel, Sharron. *The Latest and Greatest Read-Alouds.* Libraries Unlimited, 1994.

This book includes a scope and sequence, tips for reading aloud, reading early and often, lists of picture book titles, and a list of book titles beyond picture books. The last section goes further than reading aloud and provides 21 steps to building a family/classroom of readers. It also contains a complete index of titles by author, title, and subject.

Moeller, M. and V. *Middle School English Teacher's Guide to Active Learning.* Eye on Education, 2000.

The didactic and the Socratic models of teaching begin the discussion of teaching. The book continues with a conversation about active and close reading—the purpose of which is reading to interpret or to pay attention not only to what the author has to say but also how he or she says it. What does it say? What does it mean? Is it true? There are three kinds of questions: factual, interpretive, and evaluation. The theory behind active learning is explained, and sample lessons feature questions on various books, including *The Chocolate War, The Giver, Of Mice and Men,* and *The Little Prince.*

Neamen, Mimi, and Mary Strong. *Literature Circles: Cooperative Learning for Grades 3-8.* Teacher Ideas Press, 1992.

Furnished here are step-by-step instructions on how to teach with literature circles using 30 different popular novels and six picture books. For each title the authors provide a summary, vocabulary, and many ideas for projects.

Noe, Katherine L. Schlick, and Nancy J. Johnson. *Getting Started with Literature Circles.* Christopher-Gordon Publishers, 1999.

This is from the Bill Harp Professional Teachers Library series. It is short and concise—filled with lots of practical help for setting up literature circles. The topics include building a framework, classroom climate, structure, good books for literature circles, discussion, response journals, focus lessons, and extension projects.

Peterson, Ralph, and Maryann Eeds. *Grand Conversations: Literature Groups in Action.* Scholastic, 1990.

The authors discuss teaching with real books and describe a true literature-based reading program. Literary elements are highlighted, and the book concludes with some sample forms, references, and book lists.

Reuter, Janet. *Creative Teaching Through Picture Books for Middle School Students.* Frank Schaffer, 1993.

This book contains reproducible activity sheets for 27 picture books. The lessons provide lists of things to do and talk about for each book.

Rosenblatt, Louise. *The Reader, The Text, The Poem: The Transactional Theory of the Literary Work.* Southern Illinois University Press, 1978.

This is Rosenblatt's premier work on the transactional theory of reading. A text is simply words, paper, and ink until the reader makes it a literacy work. The reader reacts differently in efferent and aesthetic reading. The reading of any work is an individual and unique experience involving the mind and emotions of each reader.

Roser, Nancy, and Miriam Martinez, eds. *Book Talk and Beyond: Children and Teachers Respond to Literature.* International Reading Association, 1995.

Over 40 contributors writing 21 articles concerning book discussions make this a very useful reference volume. The articles include getting ready for book talk, the tools, leading the discussions, and responding to literature.

Routman, Regie. *Conversations: Strategies for Teaching, Learning, and Evaluating.* Heinemann, 2000.

Fifteen chapters on literacy provide information about the teacher as a professional; the literacy program; teaching children to read; encouraging children to discuss their reading; writing, journals, spelling, and word study; reading nonfiction; effective questioning; collaboration; and evaluation. The book also contains an extensive section of blue pages—resources for teachers.

Ryan, Connie. *Hooked on Books: A Genre-Based Guide for 30 Adolescent Books.* Frank Schaffer, 1993.

The author provides lists of award-winning books for adolescents, addresses of publishers, and reproducible pages for working with five books in each of these six categories: contemporary realistic fiction, adventure, fantasy and science fiction, historical fiction, mystery and suspense, and multicultural. Each lesson covers author information, story summary, background knowledge, vocabulary, discussion, and writing topics.

Saunders, Sheryl Lee. *Look and Learn! Using Picture Books in Grades Five through Eight.* Heinemann, 1999.

The introduction makes a case for the effective use of picture books for older readers. There are six chapters with four or five picture books featured in each. They include war and conflict: historical fiction; by word of mouth: traditional literature; beyond Shel and Jack: poetry; other people's lives: biography; science is a way of knowing: nonfiction; and potpourri: one-of-a-kind books. The conclusion is a guide for selecting picture books and a bibliography.

Soter, Anna. *Young Adult Literature and the New Library Theories: Developing Critical Readers in the Middle School.* Teachers College Press, 2000.

The first chapter shares alternative approaches to teaching young adult fiction. The author looks seriously at using young adult literature in the classroom and at methods of "teaching" it by recognizing that the manner in which students connect with a story is often overlooked in literature classes. The remaining chapters focus on young adult titles, including *The Island, Homecoming, My Brother Sam Is Dead, Where the Lilies Bloom, The True Confessions of Charlotte Doyle, Somewhere in the Darkness,* and *Requiem.* It concludes with a chapter on responses.

Web Sites

Children's Literature Resources
   http://fac-staff.seattleu.edu/kschlnoe/childlitlinks_copy.html

Literature Circles
   http://www.geocities.com/Wellesley/Atrium/1783/LiteratureCircles.html

Literature Circles
   http://www.sasked.gov.sk.ca/docs/mla/circle/intro.html

Literature Circles
   http://toread.com/strategies.html

Literature Circles—4th Grade
   http://mohost.moric.org/title3/learn/litcirc.htm

Literature Circles—Discussion Groups
   http://www.mcps.k12.md.us/curriculum/english/elg_lit_circles.htm

Literature Circles—Harvey Daniels
   http://www.literaturecircles.com/

Literature Circles Resource Center
   http://fac-staff.seattleu.edu/kschlnoe/LitCircles/index.html

Literature Circles—Written by Students—On Specific Titles
   http://nths.nttc.org/academics/faculty/manterfield/literature_circles.htm

Teaching Resources—Literature Circles
   http://home.att.net/~teaching/litlessons.htm

Themed Literature Units
   http://fac-staff.seattleu.edu/kschlnoe/TLU.html

7
Book Clubs

Most of the following information about book clubs is taken from our books *The Reading Connection: Bringing Parents, Teachers, and Librarians Together* (E. Knowles and M. Smith, Libraries Unlimited, 1997) and *More Reading Connections: Bringing Parents, Teachers, and Librarians Together* (E. Knowles and M. Smith, Libraries Unlimited, 1999). A book club is only as strong and dynamic as the moderators and members. Look around at school and choose a fellow faculty member you would like to work with, one who shares your love for and commitment to reading. Once you have established your meeting format and who your members will be, split the responsibilities and launch your program.

Where should the meetings be held? Your site should be centrally located and convenient. We selected our school library.

What is the best time for your club to meet? The time would depend on your target group. Working parents might find early evening or Saturday morning convenient. If you are including teachers and students, after school might be better. Our group met first thing in the morning on a Wednesday. Your parents' association might be helpful in selecting a time.

How long should the meetings last? We found that they lasted about an hour and 15 minutes, which was about all the time we could spare from our regular schedule.

How often should you meet? To begin, we suggest meeting five or six times a year. A five-month schedule might include October, November, February, March, and April. The sixth month could be either September or May. We tried to avoid the beginning of school and the busy time toward the end of the school year.

Moderator Responsibilities

1. Be familiar with the books in the topic.

2. Prepare additional discussion questions.

3. Have handouts and bibliographies included in this book ready for the book club meetings.

4. Know some interesting facts about selected authors, books, and genre.

5. Include current clippings or controversial articles appropriate to present or previous topics.

6. Distribute flyers and reminders.

7. Provide necessary books.

8. Provide coffee and refreshments.

9. READ and have FUN!

Member Responsibilities

1. Take notes as you read.

2. Respond to the guided reading questions.

3. Share your feelings and experiences.

4. Read a book to a child.

5. Attend meetings and be an active participant.

6. READ and have FUN!

How do you get the word out? We picked the dates ahead of time so they could be included in the school calendar and the information given out by the parents' association. Advertise throughout the school and introduce the program at Back to School Night or Open House as well as the first parents' association meeting. Send out invitations to prospective club members and suggest that they bring a friend. If the group is small at first, do not be discouraged, the word will spread and the group will grow.

Comments from Parents

"It is good to have guidelines when choosing books for the kids to read. Time is limited so you want them to read worthwhile books."

"The handouts were excellent, very informational for future use."

"It was a wonderful year of meetings."

"The meetings were informative. I also enjoyed the camaraderie of meeting other parents who were interested in reading and education. I enjoyed familiarizing myself with the quality books available to my children."

Frequently Asked Questions
about Book Clubs

What about the first topic? Select one of the sessions you like and are enthusiastic about. We usually started our club in October and began with Horror for Kids. This topic was timely and generated a great deal of interest and curiosity.

How do you get books to the parents? For the first session, we set aside books in the library, three weeks in advance, for the topic we had chosen. We notified the parents that they could come and check out the books they would like to read, or we would select some books and send them home with their son or daughter. This procedure is necessary only for the first meeting. Thereafter, books for the next session should be available at the end of every session. Thus the books discussed that day are returned for books on the next topic. Often parents checked out different books from the topic just discussed as well as books on the new topic.

What happens at the initial meeting? At the first meeting provide name tags and have everyone introduce themselves, including the moderators. Briefly describe the club's purposes and benefits. Provide coffee and refreshments in an informal atmosphere. Push tables together or form a circle. Keep it light and fun.

What is the format of the meetings? The moderators should see that all members participate. After a quick update on the previous session, introduce the topic for the present session. Ask each member to comment on the books just read. Usually this is all it takes, but have some discussion questions ready in case of a lull. Draw out those members who tend to sit back. Do not allow any one member to dominate the discussion. Highlight some books in the bibliography included herein, and choose those titles that are appropriate for your group. Distribute handouts at the beginning of your meeting. These might include the overview, journal article, annotated journal articles, annotated bibliography, and bibliography. Close each session with a summary of the present topic and a brief introduction to the next topic. Introduce a few books, hand out the guided reading questions, and you are on your way.

How can you acquire the books needed for your book club? There are many ways to acquire books. The following ideas were used to enhance our library and classroom collections.

Library Gift Book Program

At the beginning of the school year, send or hand out a general flyer explaining the program to all parents. Interested parents make a specified donation to the library, and the person honored is the first to take out the gift book. The funds generated cover the cost of the entire program, including preselected books and stationery. A bookplate is placed in the book to mark the occasion. The honored person is given a bookmark inscribed with his or her name and the occasion as a reminder of the donated book.

Possible gift book suggestions are numerous. We have even had a book donated in honor of a new family member—a puppy! Some suggestions include the following:

In Memory Of

Have a Great School Year

Congratulations on a Good Year

Happy Valentine's Day—I love you!
    (A small red heart was affixed to the bookplate and bookmark.)

To a Special Teacher

Merry Christmas

Happy Hanukkah

This is a very successful program. Solicit two or three reliable parents from the parents' association to organize and supervise the mailings and paperwork.

Bookshare Book Fair

The Bookshare Book Fair runs like any other book fair, with the exception that students and parents provide the books sold. Three weeks prior to the book fair students bring in books they no longer want or have outgrown. Books are sorted by age group and checked for appropriateness. All books are sold for 50 cents each, regardless of whether they are paperback or hardcover. The book fair is held in the library with the understanding that the library staff may select those books that would enhance the school's collection.

We hold this function twice a year, once in the fall and once in the spring. The biggest problem we have is the storage of books prior to the book fair. Because we tended to receive a large number of books for the very young child, we invited the local nursery schools to come and buy on the last day of the book fair. Unsold books were either saved for the next book fair or donated to appropriate local charities. This worthwhile program enhanced the library's collection and placed recycled books in the hands of many, many children.

School Book Clubs

School book clubs are another source of books and are worth the record keeping. They are a source of less expensive books. If you are concerned that some of your children are unable to purchase books, then try using your bonus points for extra books. Book clubs are a good source for multiple copies of a particular book or a set of books related to one of the sessions.

Civic Organizations

Identify community sponsors and civic groups for grant money or donations. Some organizations to consider are Kiwanis, Junior League, Rotary, public libraries, local businesses, neighborhood associations, and your school parents' association. A letter or a personal visit from the moderators may be most effective. Let the organization know that their support will be gratefully acknowledged on all handouts.

Book Clubs As Part of the Literature Program

Book clubs can be implemented in the classroom as part of the literature program. They include reading, writing, instruction, and community share. The emphasis is on discussion rather than comprehension questions, reading response journals rather than worksheets, and speaking and listening rather than seatwork. In community share the entire class meets to discuss common issues and themes from books they have read.

Professional Discussion Questions

1. Which type of book club would work best in our community? Mother/daughter? Father/son? Teachers? Teachers/students? Grade level? Parents?

2. What are ways in which we can get multiple copies of good titles?

3. Who can we count on to support us in this effort?

4. What would be the benefits we would derive from these groups for our school community?

Practical Application

Sample Topics for Book Club Sessions

The following list of sample topics is taken from *The Reading Connection: Bringing Parents, Teachers, and Librarians Together* (E. Knowles and M. Smith, Libraries Unlimited, 1997).

Sure Hits to Read Aloud

Horror for Kids

Historical Fiction

Picture Books for Young and Old

Multicultural Literature

All Kinds of Poetry

Science Fiction and Fantasy

Nonfiction and Reference

Bibliotherapy and Problem Books

Award Books

Biographies Shape Your Future

Series for Everyone

The list that follows here is taken from *More Reading Connections: Bringing Parents, Teachers, and Librarians Together* (E. Knowles and M. Smith, Libraries Unlimited, 1999).

Connecting to the Arts

Is There Truth in Humor?

Families in Transition

Social Issues . . . Too Graphic?

Folklore and Mythology—Literature of the Fireside

Predictable Sports Fiction

Many Modern Magazines for Kids

The Fine Art of Picture Books

Selection or Censorship?

Link to the Internet

Middle School Challenge

Is There Gender Bias in Children's Literature?

Whet Their Appetites with Booktalks

Our books contain all you need in order to run successful book clubs using the preceding topics. We include an overview, group discussion questions, a reprinted journal article, annotated journal articles, annotated children's books, and a bibliography of children's titles for each book club topic listed.

Young Adult Selections

Titles to Get You Started

Avi. *The True Confessions of Charlotte Doyle*. Orchard Books, 1990.

Bunting, Eve. *S.O.S. Titanic*. Harcourt Brace Juvenile Books, 1996.

Byars, Betsy. *The Pinballs*. Harper & Row, 1977.

Cooper, Susan. *The Boggart*. Margaret K. McElderry, 1993.

George, Jean Craighead. *Julie of the Wolves*. Harper & Row, 1972.

Jenkins, Steve. *The Top of the World: Climbing Mount Everest*. Houghton Mifflin Company, 1999.

Lowry. Lois. *Number the Stars*. Houghton Mifflin Company, 1989.

Naylor, Phyllis Reynolds. *The Fear Place*. Atheneum Books for Young Readers, 1994.

Rawls, Wilson. *The Summer of the Monkeys*. Bantam Doubleday Dell Books for Young Readers, 1992.

Annotated Young Adult Titles

Bauer, Joan. *Squashed*. Delacorte Press, 1992.

In Iowa, 16-year-old Ellie is trying to grow a prize-winning pumpkin. She names it Max and to her father's distress, spends too much time with the pumpkin. Ellie's mother had passed away a long time ago, and Ellie's grandmother tries to help bring her up. Ellie learns a lot about friends, struggles with her weight, and gets a boyfriend while taking care of Max.

Krisher, Trudy. *Spite Fences*. Laurel-Leaf Books, 1994.

Maggie Pugh lives in Kinship, Georgia. She receives her first camera from Zeke, who buys and sells his wares on the main street. The camera allows Maggie to see beyond the lens into the thoughts and hearts of her family and people she grew up with—both black and white. Zeke also is instrumental in getting Maggie a job cleaning house for George Hardy, a black civil rights lawyer who lives outside of town. During the summer of 1960 Maggie witnesses an inhumane act inflicted upon Zeke, initiated by her neighbor Vigil Boggs. It is a summer of civil rights and resistance, and Maggie is key to the changes ahead.

Yolen, Jane, and Bruce Coville. *Armageddon Summer*. Harcourt Brace, 1998.
  Their parents drag Marina and Jed to the mountain retreat of Reverend Beelson to wait for Armageddon—July 27, 2000.

Leaders As Readers Teachers' Book Club— Suggested Titles

Avi. *Nothing but the Truth*. Orchard Books, 1991.

Danziger, Paula. *The Cat Ate My Gymsuit*. Demco Paper, 1998.

Duncan, Lois. *Who Killed My Daughter?* Dell Publishing, 1994.

Fletcher, Ralph. *Fig Pudding*. Clarion Books, 1995.

Hesse, Karen. *Out of the Dust*. Scholastic Incorporated, 1997.

Jiang, Ji-li. *Red Scarf Girl*. HarperCollins Children's Book Group, 1997.

Kehret, Peg. *Small Steps: The Year I Got Polio*. Albert Whitman & Company, 1996.

Levitin, Sonia. *Annie's Promise*. Atheneum Books for Young Readers, 1993.

Mahmoody, Betty. *Not Without My Daughter*. St. Martin's Press, 1988.

Myers, Walter Dean. *Fallen Angels*. Scholastic Incorporated, 1988.

Nix, Garth. *Sabriel*. HarperCollins Children's Book Group, 1996.

Paulsen, Gary. *Night John*. Delacorte Press, 1993.

Annotated Titles for Leaders As Readers Teachers' Book Club

Gantos, Jack. *Joey Pigza Swallowed the Key*. Farrar Straus and Giroux, 1998.
  "Joey Pigza is wired. Really wired." Joey's actions are unpredictable and spontaneous. When he is on medication, Joey is focused, but when it is no longer effective he may swallow his household key or walk on the highest beam in a barn during a school field trip. Because Joey is endangering himself and others, he is sent to the Lancaster County Special Education Center for further evaluation. Will Joey get the help he needs for his physical and mental well being? Will he ever return to regular school?

Rennison, Louise. *Angus, Thongs and Full-Frontal Snogging: Confessions of Georgia Nicolson*. HarperCollins Children's Book Group, 2000.
  This is 14-year-old Georgia's diary—a minute-by-minute snapshot of her life, complete with all the trimmings. She has a 3-year-old sister, a cat who is prone to "leg-shredding," and embarrassing parents. She is self-conscious and struggling with the issues all teens deal with: boys, her appearance, friends, school, parents. The book is written by a British author, but there is a glossary in the back of the book to help with some of the strange terms—for example, snogging is "kissing."

Strasser, Todd. *The Wave.* Laurel-Leaf Books, 1981.

Ben Ross is an excellent teacher, but he may lose his job if his experiment fails. He conceived of "the wave" to show his history students what life would have been like in Nazi Germany. The students did not think such horror could happen again. Ben quickly demonstrates that the potential for fascism is in all of us. The experiment worked so well that even Ben was caught up in it. Now he has to figure out a way to have the students choose to end the experiment.

Annotated Suggested Professional Books for Leaders As Readers Teachers' Book Club

Beers, Kylene, and Barbara Samuels, eds. *Into Focus: Understanding and Creating Middle School Readers.* Christopher-Gordon, 1998.

There are 22 essays in this volume written by 27 authors on a wide variety of topics of interest to those working with middle school students. The topics include understanding middle school students, choosing not to read, gifted middle school readers, struggling readers, reader response theory, thematic units and readers workshop, literature discussions, literature circles, journals, content area reading, authentic reading assessment, short stories, novels, and reading and the Internet.

Roser, Nancy, and Miriam Martinez, eds. *Book Talk and Beyond: Children and Teachers Respond to Literature.* International Reading Association, 1995.

Forty contributors write 21 articles about leading book discussions. The articles include getting ready for booktalk, the tools, leading the discussions, and responding to literature.

Simmons, John, and Lawrence Baines. *Language Study in Middle School, High School, and Beyond: Views on Enhancing the Study of Language.* International Reading Association, 1998.

Ten chapters, each by different authors, discuss language study in the contemporary classroom, whole language, poetry, linguistics, sociolinguistics, reading and writing in the shadow of film and television, and the future of the written word.

Suggested Titles for Fathers and Sons Book Club

Avi. *S.O.R. Losers.* Morrow Avon, 1986.

Bloor, Edward. *Tangerine.* Harcourt Brace Juvenile Books, 1997.

Carter, Alden R. *Between a Rock and a Hard Place.* Scholastic Incorporated, 1995.

Dygard, Thomas. *River Danger.* William Morrow & Company, 1998.

Hobbs, Will. *Bearstone.* Macmillan Publishing Company, 1989.

———. *Beardance.* Atheneum Books for Young Readers, 1993.

Lawrence, Iain. *The Wreckers.* Delacorte Press, 1998.

Lynch, Chris. *Slot Machine.* HarperCollins Children's Book Group, 1995.

Mazer, Harry. *Snow Bound: A Story of Raw Survival.* Dell Paper, 1975.

Paulsen, Gary. *Hatchet.* Bradbury Press, 1987.

———. *The River.* Delacorte Press, 1991.

———. *Brian's Winter.* Delacorte Press, 1996.

———. *Puppies, Dogs, and Blue Northers.* Harcourt Brace Juvenile Books, 1996.

Sachar, Louis. *Holes.* Farrar Straus and Giroux, 1998.

Soto, Gary. *Buried Onions.* Harcourt Brace Juvenile Books, 1997.

Spinelli, Jerry. *Crash.* Alfred A. Knopf, 1996.

Annotated Suggested Titles for Fathers and Sons Book Club

McCaughrean, Geraldine. *The Pirate's Son.* Scholastic Incorporated, 1996.

Nathan Gull is penniless after his reverend father dies. He is thrown out of school and is befriended by Tamo White, a pirate's son.

Nathan and sister Maud decide to leave England and accompany Tamo back to Madagascar. They leave with Captain Sheller, Tamo's remaining guardian. Thomas White, a legendary pirate, had sent Tamo to England to school and mysteriously died shortly after.

Captain Sheller delivers the three children to Madagascar but not before he shows that everything is for sale, including Maud and the trusted navigator Hardcastle. This swashbuckling tale includes bravery, deception, strange customs, and a satisfying ending.

Ritter, John H. *Choosing Up Sides.* Philomel Books, 1998.

Luke was the son of the Holy River Baptizers' preacher. His family was sent to Crown Falls on the Ohio River bordering West Virginia during the 1920s. Luke's father believes "the left side has always been the side of Satan, contrary to God." When Luke was younger, Pa strapped his left arm to his body until it went numb, but this trained him to be right-handed. He was punished any time he used his left hand. One day, Luke stops to watch a baseball game. The ball rolls to Luke, and he easily throws it back to the bases left-handed. That pitch changes everything for Luke. He wants to play ball, to pitch, but he knows that his father thinks baseball is nothing but the Devil's playground. Will Luke convince his hot-tempered father that one has to be true to one's nature? That it is useless to try to change one's nature, just as you cannot turn the great Ohio River around?

Spinelli, Jerry. *Crash.* Alfred A. Knopf, 1996.

John Coogan is a football jock. Crash is his nickname. Penn Webb, a Quaker, is his neighbor and the target of his animosity. In seventh grade, Crash and his best friend, Mike, become the stars of the football team. They make life miserable for Penn, who is a vegetarian and a cheerleader. Crash begins to have compassion for Penn after his grandfather's illness and a cruel trick played by Mike. These two events teach Crash the value of family and true friendship.

Suggested Titles for
Mothers and Daughters Book Club

Avi. *Poppy*. Orchard Books, 1995.

Bauer, Joan. *Rules of the Road*. Putnam Publishing Group, 1998.

Bawden, Nina. *Granny the Pag*. Clarion Books, 1996.

Cushman, Karen. *Catherine Called Birdy*. Clarion Books, 1994.

———. *The Midwife's Apprentice*. Clarion Books, 1995.

———. *The Ballad of Lucy Whipple*. Clarion Books, 1996.

Fenner, Carol. *Yolanda's Genius*. Margaret K. McElderry, 1995.

Fitzhugh, Louise. *Harriet the Spy*. Harper & Row, 1964.

Freedman, Russell. *Eleanor Roosevelt: A Life of Discovery*. Clarion Books, 1993.

Hesse, Karen. *Letters from Rifka*. Henry Holt & Company, 1992.

Koningsburg, E. L. *From the Mixed-Up Files of Mrs. Basil E. Frankweiler*. Atheneum Books for Young Readers, 1967.

L'Engle, Madeleine. *A Wrinkle in Time*. Farrar Straus and Giroux, 1962.

Rappaport, Doreen. *Living Dangerously: American Women Who Risked Their Lives for Adventure*. HarperCollins Children's Book Group, 1991.

Raskin, Ellen. *The Westing Game*. Dutton Children's Books, 1978.

Taylor, Theodore. *The Trouble with Tuck*. Doubleday, 1981.

Voigt, Cynthia. *Izzy, Willy-Nilly*. Macmillan Publishing Company, 1986.

Annotated Suggested Titles for
Mothers and Daughters Book Club

Myers, Walter Dean. *At Her Majesty's Request: An African Princess in Victorian England*. Scholastic Incorporated, 1999.

Sarah Forbes Bonnetta, 5 years old, watched in horror as her family and village were destroyed. She has been captive for two years and is to be sacrificed at a special holiday ceremony by the Dahomans and King Gezo. Captain Forbes, a British naval officer who is in attendance, states that his queen (Victoria) would "never kill an innocent child and would not respect him [King Gezo] if he did so." King Gezo, King of the Blacks, gives Sarah to Victoria, Queen of the Whites. Queen Victoria accepts the unusual gift, and Sarah falls under the queen's protection and receives special attention throughout her life.

Namioka, Lensey. *Ties That Bind, Ties That Break*. Delacorte Press, 1999.

Ailin is fighting a quiet war against Chinese tradition. When she was 5, her mother and grandmother tried on several occasions to bind her feet. Ailin refuses and her father agrees and feels that the old customs will fade. She is too young to understand the consequences. Her arranged engagement is broken, and at 14 years old she is forced to leave home with few options. She becomes a nanny for a missionary family, which is beneath the well-educated young Chinese woman. Ailin dresses in Western clothing and is taken for a foreigner in her own country. Through hard work and courage, Ailin finds happiness and acceptance in America. A note on the Chinese tradition of footbinding is included.

Thomas, Jane Resh. *Behind the Mask: The Life of Queen Elizabeth I.* Clarion Books, 1998.

Queen Elizabeth I displayed the image of Gloriana, good Queen Bess, or the Virgin Queen wedded to her subjects as the situation required. Elizabeth lived her entire life threatened by death. She became a queen in an age when women were considered morally weak and less capable than men. For this reason and the fact that she had no heir, Parliament demanded that she marry. Elizabeth gave the appearance that she was seeking a suitable husband, but she preferred being single and queen. Elizabeth dramatically removed her coronation ring from her finger "Behold . . . the Pledge of this my Wedlock and Marriage with my Kingdom." Elizabeth protected England from religious and foreign foes and defeated the Spanish Armada. "The little second-rate kingdom that she inherited had grown into a respectable power, and its reviled queen had gained the esteem of the mighty. Elizabeth dominated the sixteenth century, and she is honored by hers being called the Elizabethan Age.

Annotated Professional Journal Articles

Burstein, Sharon. "Where Everyone's Turned On to Reading," *Teaching K-8* (May 1999): 56-57.

Once a month, students and parents meet after school with refreshments to discuss a selected book. Anyone may join the group regardless of grade or reading ability. Members of the community are also invited to participate. If you are interested in organizing a local book club, contact your Rotary Club or a similar organization for assistance.

Giorgis, Cyndi, Nancy J. Johnson, Chrissie Colbert, Angela Conner, Abby Franklin, and Janine King. "What Makes a Good Book?" *The Reading Teacher* (December/January 1999/2000): 344-51.

The books reviewed in this column reflect the many reasons for choosing a book to read. Included were books that

- ◄◄ withstood the test of time,
- ◄◄ related to a common experience,
- ◄◄ extended knowledge,
- ◄◄ inspired readers to follow their dreams, and
- ◄◄ invited readers back again and again.

All were chosen because they were memorable—simply put, "good books."

Madison, Katie O'Dell. "You Go Girl: A Road Map to Girl Power," *VOYA* (June 1999): 92-95.

This article summarizes "girl power" resources that a library might be interested in. It includes books, magazines, web sites, and national organizations to help empower individual girls in their YA years.

Mather, Becky. "Read n' Rap: Connecting Girls through Literature and Technology," *The Book Report* (January/February 2000): 19-20.

Read n' Rap is a collaborative project between fifth grade and high school girls. The students read age-appropriate literature and discuss books and their reactions to them via e-mail. High school girls act as mentors to younger girls through guiding questions and follow-up discussions. Future plans include expanding the program to include other schools, using the literature circles discussion model in fifth grade, and posting all discussions on a moderated listserv. Read n' Rap provides a positive role model for adolescent girls.

McDermott, Cynthia, and Suzanne Gemmell. "Fathers and Sons," *Book Links* (September 1996): 42-48.

Fathers should be encouraged to read to their children—especially their male children. It is important for children to see male role models reading. Invite male family members, men of the community, and male teachers or staff to read to the children. And what should they read? An annotated bibliography of picture books and novels is included to get started.

Moore, Nancy Jane. "We Were Reading Geography Books! I Thought We Were Reading for Fun: Parents and a Librarian Take on Seventh Grade Book Groups," *VOYA* (December 1999): 310-11.

One parent was the incentive behind dividing 175 seventh graders into book groups of 10, which met every Friday for six months. Fifteen paperback titles were selected that dealt with the Eastern Hemisphere and initiated good discussions. The groups moved at different rates, but they tried to switch the books every two to four weeks. Some of the books were matched with films as a variation. Students voted for their favorite books, and the results, as well as student comments, are included in this article.

Odean, Kathleen. "Dynamic Older Women," *Book Links* (May 1997): 34-36.

The author annotates many picture books that have dynamic older women as alternatives to the "little old lady" stereotype. These picture books could be used with older students as good discussion starters.

Raphael, Taffy E., and Susan I. McMahon. "Book Club: An Alternative Framework for Reading Instruction," *The Reading Teacher* (October 1994): 102-15.

The book club program "integrates reading, writing, student-led discussion groups, whole-class discussions, and instruction." Many positive changes in student behaviors and abilities were observed as they became more experienced using the book club program. Earlier conversations were shallow and followed the classroom rules of taking turns rather than authentic conversations. Students learned to develop sequence charts to enhance their understanding, generate various types of questions for discussion, and analyze literary elements. By using this model of reading instruction the authors "learned the importance of integrating reading within the language arts since both discussion and writing promoted students' reading and interpretation of texts."

Ward, Caroline. "Having Their Say: How to Lead Great Book Discussions with Children," *School Library Journal* (April 1998): 24-29.

Libraries should capitalize on the book club trend and offer book club discussions once a month at different grade levels. The author has compiled some points to consider in selecting books; the factual, interpretive, and evaluative types of questions; and how to facilitate a discussion. The article includes the ABCs of book discussion, leading questions, and ways to spark discussion.

Annotated Professional Books

Bauermeister, Erica, and Holly Smith. *Let's Hear It for the Girls: 375 Great Books for Readers 2-14.* Penguin, 1997.

This book is divided by age levels, and each book annotation is quite complete. The titles are listed by subject, author, genre, and publication date.

Dodson, Shireen. *100 Books for Girls to Grow On.* HarperCollins, 1998.

From the author of *The Mother-Daughter Book Club,* all entries in this book are arranged alphabetically by title, and each includes a summary, reading time, themes, discussion questions, author information, beyond the book, and if you liked this book try . . .

Drew, Bernard. *The 100 Most Popular Young Adult Authors: Biographical Sketches and Bibliographies.* Libraries Unlimited, 1997.

Authors are listed alphabetically, and there is a short biography and information on all the various types of writing each author has produced.

Herald, Diana. *Teen Genreflecting.* Libraries Unlimited, 1997.

This book begins with a section on teen genre fiction, including the nature of it, cover art and format, reviews, programs for teens, and resources for librarians. Next it contains chapters on historical novels, science fiction, fantasy, mystery and suspense, adventure, contemporary, and romance. Each chapter includes long lists of briefly annotated titles subdivided into topics.

Jody, Marilyn, and Marianne Saccardi. *Using Computers to Teach Literature: A Teacher's Guide.* National Council of Teachers of English, 1998.

This resource discusses the BookRead Project and connects classes and authors for online discussions of literature. It has an annotated list of language arts web sites, author web sites, publishers' sites, staff development online, and books online. There are excerpts from online author chats and chats about certain readings. It concludes with an annotated bibliography of children's books and resources for teachers.

Kaywell, Joan, ed. *Adolescent Literature as a Complement to the Classics, Volume 4.* Christopher-Gordon, 2000.

This book is divided by chapters on classic titles with connections to current young adult literature. The premise is that classics will be easier to understand and perhaps better accepted by adolescents if there is a connection to current literature. The classics discussed are *Our Town, Oliver Twist, The Crucible, My Antonia, A Lesson Before Dying, The Call of the Wild, The Hunchback of Notre Dame, Henry IV, Pride and Prejudice, I Heard the Owl Call My Name, The Once and Future King, The Dark Is Rising* series, *Cyrano de Bergerac, The Tragedy of Dr. Faustus,* and *Antigone.*

Knowles, E., and M. Smith. *The Reading Connection: Bringing Parents, Teachers, and Librarians Together.* Libraries Unlimited, 1997.

Establishing a book club is a great way to involve parents in promoting literacy to young readers. This book shows you how to start a book club in your school or community, and it provides bibliographies of literature resources for children in grades K through 8. Suggested topics and sample book club sessions help you get started, and the extensive bibliography, arranged by genre, can guide parents and students in selecting reading material. Chapters cover read-alouds, picture books, horror stories, multicultural literature, poetry, science fiction, nonfiction and reference, bibliotherapy and problem novels, award-winning books, biographies, and books in a series. For each genre the authors offer a general overview, suggest discussion questions, provide a bibliography, and list resources for further reading. Helpful Internet addresses and additional topics are included in the concluding chapter.

Knowles, E., and M. Smith. *More Reading Connections: Bringing Parents, Teachers, and Librarians Together.* Libraries Unlimited, 1999.

Great topics and sample book club sessions help you start a book club and keep it going! Chapters in this volume cover humor, families, social issues, folklore and mythology, sports, magazines, picture books as art, censorship, the Internet, middle school readers, gender bias, booktalks, and the arts. For each genre the authors offer a general overview, discussion questions, a bibliography, resources for further reading, and appropriate web sites. If you want to promote literacy and involve parents in the reading program, you'll love this book and its companion, *The Reading Connection.*

McElmeel, Sharron. *The Latest and Greatest Read-Alouds.* Libraries Unlimited, 1994.

The author provides a scope and sequence, tips for reading aloud, reading early and often, lists of picture book titles, and a list of titles beyond picture books. The last section is going beyond reading aloud and 21 steps to building a family/classroom of readers. It also includes a complete index of titles by author, title, and subject.

Odean, Kathleen. *Great Books for Girls: More Than 600 Books to Inspire Today's Girls and Tomorrow's Women.* Ballantine Books, 1997.

These annotated books for girls are grouped by picture books; folktales; books for beginning readers, middle readers, and older readers; and resources for parents.

Peterson, Ralph, and Maryann Eeds. *Grand Conversations: Literature Groups in Action.* Scholastic, 1990.

The authors discuss teaching with real books and describe a true literature-based reading program. Literary elements are highlighted, and the book concludes with some sample forms, references, and booklists.

Raphael, T., L. Pardo, K. Highfield, and S. McMahon. *Book Club: A Literature-Based Curriculum.* Small Planet Communications, 1997.

A video is included with this book. The first portion of the book describes the book club program, including classroom management, assessment, and teaching tips. Next there are lesson plans for eight specific titles, an author study, and five multi-book units. There is also a section of additional resources, including reproducible think sheets and assessment forms. This is an excellent resource for starting book discussions as an integral part of a literature program.

Routman, Regie. *Conversations: Strategies for Teaching, Learning, and Evaluating.* Heinemann, 2000.

Fifteen chapters on literacy provide information about the teacher as a professional; the literacy program; teaching children to read; encouraging children to discuss their reading; writing; journals; spelling and word study; reading nonfiction; effective questioning; collaboration; and evaluation. The book also contains a large section of blue pages—resources for teachers.

Ryan, Connie. *Hooked on Books: A Genre-Based Guide for 30 Adolescent Books.* Frank Schaffer, 1993.

Hooked on Books furnishes lists of award-winning books for adolescents, addresses of publishers, and reproducible pages for working with five books in each of the following six categories: contemporary realistic fiction, adventure, fantasy and science fiction, historical fiction, mystery and suspense, and multicultural. Each lesson includes author information, story summary, background knowledge, vocabulary, discussion, and writing topics.

Wadham, Tim and Rachel. *Bringing Fantasy Alive for Children and Young Adults.* Linworth, 1999.

The authors start with an overview of fantasy, including traditional and contemporary, children's responses, barriers to appreciating fantasy, and its literary aspects. The next section deals with practical ways to share fantasy with children, including integrating it into the curriculum through booktalks, programs, and story times. There is also an Internet section with online fantasy resources, general literature sites, author sites, and listserv discussion groups. Selected author biographies and extensive annotated lists of titles are divided by picture books, chapter books, and grade level.

Whitfield, Jamie. *Getting Kids Hooked on Literature: A Hands-On Guide to Making Literature Exciting for Kids.* Prufrock Press, 1998.

Whitfield provides four chapters: conversations, discussions, and debates; art, movies, and music; games and simulations; and reports and research. In each chapter there are three or four novels/books featured with a variety of reproducible activities and suggestions for use.

Web Sites

American Adventure Club for Ages 8-12
    http://www.cwd.com/barbour/

Article about The Teacher Book Club by Shari M. Goldberg and Ellen Pesko
    http://www.ascd.org/readingroom/edlead/0005/goldberg.html

Book Club: A Literature Based Curriculum—Includes All the Tools Needed
    http://www.smplanet.com/bookclub/bookclub.html

Book Groups for Kids
    http://www.multnomah.lib.or.us/lib/kids/mdbg.html

Collection of book clubs listed by interest
    http://www.book-clubs.com/

Index to Clubs and What They Are Reading—Mostly Adult
    http://www.bookmarc.com/Bookclub.htm

Join or Start a Reading Group with Yahoo
    http://dir.yahoo.com/Arts/Humanities/Literature/Organizations/Reading_Groups/

Oprah's Book Club Has a Kids' Reading List
    http://www.oprah.com/obc/obc_landing.html

Scholastic's Book Club Site
    http://teacher.scholastic.com/bookclubs/index.htm

Tips for Organizing a Young People's Bookgroup
    http://www.milkweed.org/6_1.html

Vintage Books Discusses Selections for Reading Groups and Useful Resources to Facilitate the Groups Discussions—Adult
    http://www.randomhouse.com/vintage/read/

8

Booktalks

Bodart (1992) describes booktalks as sales pitches for books, a brief come-on, an intriguing glimpse of what is inside, or a commercial for a book. Littlejohn (1999) says you should think of yourself as a salesperson, and you are selling the love of reading to students who are the consumers. The purpose is to stimulate reading and a love of literature through delivering tantalizing introductions to books. Booktalks can be done for all grade levels—even as low as kindergarten. Booktalks are very important for poor readers who often have a very difficult time selecting a book. Booktalks can help to expand the experiential background and knowledge of readers—they encourage continued growth in literacy.

Littlejohn (2000) is doing her doctoral dissertation on booktalking, and she makes these important points about reading:

- The more reading one does, the more skilled at reading one becomes.

- For all readers, reading development is a highly individual process.

- Students respond more positively when they know something about the book before they begin reading it.

- Lifelong readers usually develop the habit of reading long before adulthood.

- Booktalks endorse reading as a positive lifelong skill.

Teachers should booktalk classroom library books and all books assigned to be read. Booktalks can be displayed on bulletin boards and handed out as an introduction to a book to be used in class. Both books by Littlejohn, annotated at the end of this chapter, provide hundreds of actual booktalks and the author's permission to photocopy them and use them to booktalk books in your classroom. She suggests keeping a file of the ones you will use each year with your curriculum and adding as many new ones as possible. Littlejohn suggests a maximum of three minutes booktalking each book, and as many as 10 at a time!

There are two main categories of booktalks: informal and formal. The informal booktalk is a spontaneous introduction to books that might happen on any day. With the formal booktalk you know your audience—age, grade level, range of abilities and interests, levels of maturation and sophistication—and you know your books—either you have read them or used a book review journal or other secondary source. It is good to make a card file of successful booktalks. The title should be clearly stated. Give a plot summary (don't give away the plot!), key passages (from the beginning), a description of an especially interesting character or setting, the theme of book, information about the author, and other related titles. Never tell the ending. If you read a passage, make sure it is short and exciting. Props can be useful, keep the talk short, and have several copies of the book to hand out immediately to interested students.

Decide on the number of titles you will cover in your booktalk—one or two at length, or many briefly. If a large number of books are to be introduced, include a bibliography so the listeners can make note of interesting ones. This will also prevent confusion. Will there be a connecting theme? The selections should represent the interests and reading levels of the group: some difficult, some average, some easy, some old titles, some new, some fiction, some nonfiction, and so on.

Professional Discussion Questions

1. What booktalking resources are available to us?

2. Should the librarian be the only one to booktalk?

3. Why is this an important task?

4. How can we encourage students to do effective booktalks?

5. What are the benefits of booktalking?

Practical Application

Booktalk Web Site

http://rms.concord.k12.nh.us/booktalks/default.htm

Nancy Keane's Booktalks—Quick and Simple is a web site with over 700 booktalks to be used by teachers and librarians. Each one includes bibliographical information, and the titles are sorted by interest level, subject area, author, and title. Booktalking Tips, New Listings, Reading Lists, and Awards are other areas available on the site. The Booktalking Tips section features a great variety of ideas from many teachers and librarians. The site was developed by Nancy J. Keane, library media specialist at Rundlett Middle School, Concord, New Hampshire. Anyone can submit a booktalk to be included simply by e-mailing it to Ms. Keane. The following is a booktalk from the site, reprinted by permission.

Sample Booktalk (from Web Site)

Bauer, Joan
RULES OF THE ROAD
New York: Putnam, 1998.
IL YA
ISBN 0399231404
Jenna now has her driver's license and is ready to hit the road. She can't believe her luck when her boss at the shoe store asks Jenna to drive her from Chicago to Texas. Mrs. Gladstone has a little job for Jenna to do along the way. Jenna is enlisted as a corporate spy.

She is asked to spy on other shoe stores. Come get some shopping tips along the way as Jenna learns THE RULES OF THE ROAD.

SUBJECTS: Stores, Retail—Fiction
Old age—Fiction
Automobile driving—Fiction
Alcoholism—Fiction
Texas—Fiction

Suggested Young Adult Titles for Booktalks

Abelove, Joan. *Go and Come Back*. DK Incorporated, 1998.

Avi. *Beyond the Western Sea, the Escape from Home*. Orchard Books, 1996.

Blackwood, Gary. *The Shakespeare Stealer*. Dutton Children's Books, 1998.

Bloor, Edward, *Tangerine.* Harcourt Brace Juvenile Books, 1997.

Brewster, Hugh. *Anastasia's Album*. Hyperion Books for Children, 1996.

Cooney, Caroline B. *The Voice on the Radio*. Delacorte Press, 1996.

Creech, Sharon. *Chasing Redbird*. HarperCollins Children's Book Group, 1997.

Curtis, Christopher Paul. *The Watsons Go to Birmingham—1963*. Clarion Books, 1994.

Dorris, Michael. *Sees Behind Trees*. Hyperion Books for Children, 1996.

Enzensberger, Hans Magnus. *The Number Devil: A Mathematical Adventure*. Henry Holt and Company, 1998.

Farmer, Nancy. *The Ear, the Eye, and the Arm.* Orchard Books, 1994.

———. *A Girl Named Disaster*. Orchard Books, 1996.

Fleischman, Sid. *Bandit's Moon*. HarperCollins Children's Book Group, 1998.

Fletcher, Susan. *Shadow Spinner*. Simon & Schuster Books for Young Readers, 1998.

Freedman, Russell. *Martha Graham: A Dancer's Life*. Clarion Books, 1998.

Gantos, Jack. *Heads or Tails: Stories from the Sixth Grade*. Farrar Straus and Giroux, 1994.

———. *Joey Pigza Swallowed the Key*. Farrar Straus and Giroux, 1998.

Greenberg, Jan, and Sandra Jordan. *Chuck Close, Up Close*. DK Incorporated, 1998.

Griffin, Adele. *The Other Shepards*. Hyperion Books for Children, 1998.

Hahn, Mary Downing. *Following My Own Footsteps*. Clarion Books, 1996.

Henkes, Kevin. *Protecting Marie*. Greenwillow Books, 1995.

Hesse, Karen. *Music of the Dolphins*. Scholastic Incorporated, 1996.

Hobbs, Will. *Far North*. William Morrow & Company, 1996.

Holt, Kimberly Willis. *My Louisiana Sky*. Henry Holt & Company, 1998.

Konigsburg, E. L. *The View from Saturday*. Atheneum Books for Young Readers, 1996.

Lasky, Kathryn. *True North: A Novel of the Underground Railroad*. Blue Sky Press, 1996.

Lobel, Anita. *No Pretty Pictures: A Child of War*. Greenwillow Books, 1998.

McCaughrean, Geraldine. *The Pirate's Son*. Scholastic Incorporated, 1998.

McGraw, Eloise. *The Moorchild*. Simon & Schuster Books for Young Readers, 1996.

Napoli, Donna Jo. *Sirena*, Scholastic Incorporated, 1998.

Naylor, Phyllis Reynolds. *Shiloh Season*. Simon & Schuster Books for Young Readers, 1996.

Paterson, Katherine. *The Great Gilly Hopkins*. HarperCollins Children's Book Group, 1978.

Perl, Lila, and Marion Blumenthal. *Four Perfect Pebbles: A Holocaust Story*. Greenwillow Books, 1996.

Pullman, Philip. *The Golden Compass*. Alfred A. Knopf, 1996.

Reaver, Chap. *Bill*. Delacorte Press, 1994.

Roberts, Willo Davis. *Twisted Summer*. Simon & Schuster Books for Young Readers, 1996.

Sachar, Louis. *There's a Boy in the Girl's Bathroom*. Scholastic Incorporated, 1987.

Schulman, Arlene. *Muhammad Ali: Champion*. Lerner Publishing Group, 1996.

Skurzynski, Gloria. *Virtual War*. Simon & Schuster Books for Young Readers, 1997.

Sleator, William. *Interstellar Pig*. Peter Smith Publishers Incorporated, 1996.

Tanaka, Shelley. *On Board the Titanic*. Hyperion Books for Young Readers, 1998.

Taylor, Mildred D. *The Well*. Dial Books for Young Readers, 1995.

Temple, Frances. *The Ramsey Scallop*. Orchard Books, 1994.

———. *The Beduins' Gazelle*. Orchard Books, 1996.

Voigt, Cynthia. *When She Hollers*. Scholastic Incorporated, 1996.

Wick, Walter. *Walter Wick's Optical Tricks*. Scholastic Incorporated, 1998.

Wolff, Virginia Euwer. *Bat 6*. Scholastic Incorporated, 1998.

Wynne-Jones, Tim. *The Book of Changes*. Orchard Books, 1995.

———. *Some of the Kinder Planets*. Orchard Books, 1996.

Yolen, Jane. *Here There Be Ghosts*. Harcourt Brace Juvenile Books, 1998.

Annotated Young Adult Titles
for Booktalks

Bauer, Joan. *Rules of the Road.* G. P. Putnam's Sons, 1998.

Jenna works at a shoe store for the summer and her ways catch the attention of the elderly owner. She becomes the owner's driver, and they go on a 6-week trip to visit company shoe stores and keep the woman's young son from forcing her out of the business.

Bodett, Tom. *Williwaw!* Alfred A. Knopf, 1999.

This novel is by Tom Bodett of Motel 6 fame. The title *Williwaw* is a violent and unbending storm. September and her brother, Ivan, are left alone for two weeks while their father is away earning money for a new fishing boat. Ivan blows up their two radios when he wrongly tries to hook up his video games. Against their father's orders the children go to town in hopes of repairing their radios. September and Ivan find themselves in the midst of a williwaw and out of control. Will their father be able to rescue them?

DeClements, Barthe. *Liar, Liar.* Marshall Cavendish, 1998.

Gretchen Griswald lives with her dad, and her three brothers (one step-brother) live with her mom. She has a good friend named Susan November, and she gets along well at school until a new girl, Marybelle, moves in town. Marybelle starts telling tales about the teacher and classmates. Soon the girls she likes most are snubbing Gretchen. Her brother helps her get to the bottom of the problem.

Glenn, Mel. *Foreign Exchange.* Morrow Junior Books, 1999.

Students from an urban high school are invited to spend a weekend in a rural town, with each urban teen paired with a rural one. Local girl Kristen Clarke is found murdered, and the blame is placed on an urban African-American student who was dancing with her at the "foreign exchange" dance. The story is told through poetry and examines stereotypes and prejudices.

Griffin, Adele. *The Other Shepards.* Hyperion Books for Children, 1998.

Before Geneva and Holland were born, a drunk driver killed their sister and two brothers when they were teenagers. Its effects are manifested in the compulsive behaviors of sixth-grader Geneva and eighth-grader Holland. At first glance, it appears that Geneva is the one most disturbed by events she had no control over, and Holland is the older sister who looks out for her. As the story progresses, however, it is Geneva who is the key to both of the girls recovering from the strain and burden of grief that fills their lives. Through the guidance of Annie, who arrives to paint a mural in their home, the girls gradually leave the rituals behind and respond to impulses, which allow them to experience life. Is Annie an imaginary friend or the ghost of their dead sister Elizabeth Ann?

Haddix, Margaret Peterson. *Leaving Fishers.* Aladdin Paperbacks, 1997.

Dorry moved from Ohio and is new at Crestwood High. She is having a hard time adjusting until a group called the Fishers begins to invite her to sit and eat with them at school. Gradually she is doing more and more with the group and is attending their church, bible study classes, and is submitting to the strict demands of her discipler, Angela. In spite of her doubts, Dorry continues to adhere to the Fishers and donates her college fund to the church. Under pressure to convert someone, she begins to tell the children she is baby-sitting for about God and the fires of hell. This is a turning point for Dorry, and she realizes the harm she is doing to herself and family. Slowly Dorry realizes that she has been involved in a cult and was brainwashed into believing and doing what the Fishers wanted.

Jones, Diana Wynne. *Dark Lord of Derkholm.* Greenwillow Books, 1998.

The peace-loving, inventive Wizard Derek is chosen to be this year's Dark Lord. His responsibility is to oversee the evil side of the offworld Pilgrim Tours. Battles, wild hunts, pirates, enchanted spells, and an evil fortress entertain the Pilgrim parties. Everything is an illusion with some dire consequences for those deemed expendable. However, this year everything seems to be going awry. What is the real reason behind these Pilgrim Tours organized by Mr. Chesney of the other world? Why do the dragons bring their gold treasure every year to Mr. Chesney? What use does Mr. Chesney have for the mined earth of the offworld? Meet Derek's human children, his five griffin children, flying pigs, flying horses, invisible cats, intelligent geese, friendly cows, dragons, elves, and enough magic to keep one reading.

McKinley, Robin. *Spindle's End.* G. P. Putnam's Sons, 2000.

A young adult–length version of the fairy tale "Briar Rose" complete with magic, fairies, spells, and talking animals. Briar Rose, or Rosie, is a princess, and on her naming day the evil fairy Pernicia casts a spell on her that, before her 21st birthday, will cause her to be pricked by a spindle on a weaving loom and thus die. Pernicia's magic will be the strongest just before the fated birthday. Katriona, a good fairy, whisks Rosie away on her naming day and takes her home to Foggy Bottom in a remote area called the Gig. Rosie is kept safe because she is raised in ordinary circumstances, and she talks to animals as if she were a fairy. Three months before her 21st birthday, her 21st godparent, just ahead of Pernicia, finds Rosie. An elaborate disguise is planned, and Peony, who looks more like a princess than Rosie, will pretend to be the princess, and Rosie will be the lady-in-waiting. In the end, however, it will be Rosie and her beloved animals that will win over Pernicia and rid the world of her evil. By choice, Rosie never becomes a princess and returns to a simple life as the wife of a smithy. "All will be well."

Mikaelsen, Ben. *Petey.* Hyperion Books for Children, 1998.

Petey was born in the early 1920s with cerebral palsy. In those days people had no idea what it was and assumed he was an idiot. He was institutionalized after his parents could no longer care for him. Since he is unable to speak, he is wasting away in an asylum in Montana. His only contact is with an occasional few kind helpers who realize he is alert and certainly not retarded, only totally helpless in a deformed body. A young boy eventually befriends him. The boy takes him out for walks, to the movies, and helps to get him a new and better wheelchair.

Wynne-Jones, Tim. *The Maestro.* Orchard Books, 1996.

Burl Crow lives with his dysfunctional parents: a mother spaced out on drugs and a father who beats him and seems to hate him. He escapes into the wilderness and finds a cabin and a pianist-composer who is enjoying the solitude—getting away from his busy life to compose. Burl stays with him and begins a segment of his life that changes his future.

Annotated Professional Journal Articles

Bromann, Jennifer. "The Toughest Audience on Earth," *School Library Journal* (October 1999): 60-62.

Bromann shares sample booktalks and tips for effective booktalking:

◀◀ Never read from note cards.

◀◀ Convince the students you are a friend (not a teacher/librarian) sharing a book.

◀◀ Use a sarcastic and playful tone.

◀◀ Make the class the focus, not the book.

◀◀ Watch your words: "If you read this book" or, "I brought some books you may want to use if you need to do a book report or assignment."

◀◀ Don't be afraid to tease.

◀◀ Give students what they want—sex, drugs, dating, danger, and murder.

◀◀ Stretch the truth a little.

◀◀ Limit your booktalks to eight books, or not more than 15 minutes.

Edwards, Lis, Terry McConnell, and Harry Sprouse. "The Invisible School Librarian's Reappearance," *Book Report* (May/June 1999): 18-20.

High school librarians discuss three projects that involve students and teachers using the media center. The third project is student-produced video booktalks that were used in conjunction with a Great Books unit. The video booktalks were pivotal to the success of the unit.

Keane, Nancy J. "Students Take to the Airwaves to Talk Books," *Book Report* (January/February 2000): 27-28.

The author combines kids, books, and talk radio for some surprising results. *Kids Book Beat* grew out of a book club held once a week before school. Students came and discussed the books they were reading and tried to convince others to read also. From this grew the idea of a live twenty-minute booktalk show once a month, based around a theme. Another variation of this idea is a taped, edited video format of the club's book discussions.

Littlejohn, Carol. "Rebels With (and Without) a Cause: Booktalks for Grades 7-12," *The Book Report* (May/June 1998): 27-29.

This article includes a list of books suitable for booktalking on the theme of rebels in YA literature and includes a wide variety of genres and levels of reading. Littlejohn's booktalks frequently appear in *The Book Report.*

Norton, Terry L., and Carol S. Anfin. "Brush Up Your Booktalks: Promoting Literature-Based Reading: Part I," *School Library Media Activities Monthly* (November 1997): 29-32.

There are three types of booktalks. One revolves around core books; one around genre, theme, or authors; and one around self-selection of books. Booktalks provide reading guidance to students and are effective with students of low ability. Booktalks increase the library's circulation and combine the process of reading with important subject content. The authors provide tips for beginning booktalkers. This article is one of two.

Norton, Terry L., and Carol S. Anfin. "Brush Up Your Booktalks: Promoting Literature-Based Reading: Part II," *School Library Media Activities Monthly* (December 1997): 27-34.

There are four basic types of booktalks. The plot summary discusses the plot up to an exciting point and then stops. The anecdote talks about a particular scene or single incident. The character description format "lends itself to books in which a person, animal or entity is the main focus." The fourth type, creation of a mood, is often used in combination with one of the other types. A fifth type of booktalk could be based around a particular theme, author, or genre. Booktalks should be varied, entertaining, and no more than four to eight titles at a time.

Repman, Judi. "Making the Reading-Writing Connection for the 21st Century," *Library Talk* (September/October 1998): 11-13.

Use the Web to promote reading and writing skills. The author suggests several web sites that allow students to publish their own works of fiction, poetry, or wacky web tales. OGRE, the Orange Grove Review of Books, allows children to submit reviews of YA books. The Book Review Forum has a searchable database of student-written book reviews. When students are writing for their peers they tend to be more conscientious, and if they are encouraged to publish on the Web it will increase their audience.

Shoemaker, Joel. "Where Can I Get a List of Really Good Books for Teenagers?" *Book Report* (January/February 2000): 61-63.

Sites of interest to young adults and young adult librarians are discussed:

‣ http://www.ala.org/yalsa (web site of Young Adult Library Services Association) Site includes: Booklists, Alex Awards, Best Books for YA, Top 10 List, Quick Picks, Popular Paperbacks, 1999 Selected Audio Books, Michael L. Printz Award, and YALSA-BK electronic discussion list.

‣ http://www.ala.org/teenhoopla

‣ http://www.ala.org/teen-read (Teen Read Week)

Stone, Betty W. "Promoting Reading to Middle School Students: May the Booktalks Continue," *Book Report* (January/February 2000): 12-15.

Classic and current titles to use in booktalks are divided by genres: fantasy, mysteries, contemporary fiction, outdoor/adventure fiction, historical fiction, and humorous fiction. The best part of booktalking these titles is reading them first.

Annotated Professional Books

Bodart, J., ed. *The New Booktalker*, vol. 1. Libraries Unlimited, 1992.

Bodart is nationally known as the foremost authority on booktalking. Several authors have contributed articles about booktalking to the first portion, but the majority of the pages in this book contain complete booktalks on a great many titles. These booktalks are written by teachers and media specialists from across the country.

Drew, Bernard. *The 100 Most Popular Young Adult Authors: Biographical Sketches and Bibliographies.* Libraries Unlimited, 1997.

The authors are listed alphabetically, and there is short biography and information on all the various types of writing each author has produced.

Herald, Diana. *Teen Genreflecting.* Libraries Unlimited, 1997.

This book begins with a section on teen genre fiction, including the nature of it, cover art and format, reviews, programs for teens, and resources for librarians. Next, it contains chapters on historical novels, science fiction, fantasy, mystery and suspense, adventure, contemporary, and romance. Each chapter includes long lists of briefly annotated titles subdivided into topics.

Littlejohn, Carol. *Talk That Book: Booktalks to Promote Reading.* Linworth, 1999.

This is an excellent resource for booktalking. The author begins by describing booktalking as a brief commercial about a book, giving just enough information to promote reading it. It should have a catchy beginning and a cliffhanger ending, and if the talk does not spark some interest in the book, then it should be rewritten until it does. The booktalks are reproducible and divided into three sections: grades 4 through 6; 6 through 8; and 9 and up; and at the back of the book the titles are grouped by theme.

Littlejohn, Carol. *Keep Talking That Book! Booktalks to Promote Reading*, vol. 2. Linworth, 2000.

A second volume with many more short and exciting booktalks in a reproducible format so that you can make your own file of booktalks. This makes booktalking something that all teachers and librarians can do to help promote interest in reading for pleasure in the middle and high school years. The titles are grouped by level and also listed by theme. This is a resource every educator interested in stamping out aliteracy should have.

McElmeel, Sharron. *The Latest and Greatest Read-Alouds.* Libraries Unlimited, 1994.

The author provides a scope and sequence, tips for reading aloud, reading early and often, lists of picture book titles, and a list of titles beyond picture books. The last section is going beyond reading aloud and 21 steps to building a family/classroom of readers. It also includes a complete index of titles by author, title, and subject.

Web Sites

Book Reviews Written by Teens
　　http://www.ala.org/teenhoopla

Booktalks
　　http://www.washburn.edu/mabee/booktalks/booktalk.html

Cathy Young's Favorite Teenage Angst Books
　　http://www.grouchy.com/angstbooks.html

Links to Wacky Web Tales
　　http://www.eduplace.com/kids/index

Nancy J. Keane Website—Includes Nearly 700 Booktalks
　　http://www.concord.k12.nh.us/booktalks

OGRE, the Orange Grove Review of Books
　　http://www.falcon.cfsd.k12.az.us/~ogwww/reviews/ogre

Publishes Student Work
　　http://www.kidpub.org/kidpub

Reading Rants by Jennifer Hurst
　　http://www.tln.lib.mi.us/~amutch/jen

Student Written Book Reviews
　　http://www.faldo.atmos.uiuc.edu/BOOKREVIEW

Technology and Booktalks
　　http://academic.wsc.edu/redl/classes/Tami/booktalk.html

Web Site of the Young Adult Library Services Association
　　http://www.ala.org/yalsa

9

Interdisciplinary and Thematic Units

Interdisciplinary units are those that focus on making connections between subject areas. These units dissolve the normal boundaries between the disciplines. The topics can range from history, such as Ancient Egypt; science, such as wolves; a theme, such as prejudice; a genre, such as folklore; or an imaginary topic, such as dragons. All of these can be easily linked with literature. More and more emphasis has been placed on the power of literature to integrate curriculum. Linking disciplines through literature provides for a richer, more meaningful understanding of subject matter and a relevant way to introduce students to the pleasures and rewards of reading.

Roberts and Kellough (2000) say it is important for students to understand that learning is interrelated, whole, and connected, rather than a series of separate subjects or disciplines. Following individual interests can motivate learning. Linking disciplines with literature can facilitate collaborative learning as well as help students to become independent problem solvers.

Wood, Flood, and Lapp (1994) believe that integrated curriculum deliberately relates ideas rather than assuming students will make connections between disciplines. A center or project approach provides a format for linking disciplines through reading, writing, speaking, and listening on a cross-curricular topic.

Smith and Johnson (1993) explain an approach that uses literature to examine a theme that combines concerns of adolescents and world issues. This method uses primary sources rather than concentrating on fragmented subjects and content textbooks.

There are many teacher resources containing lists of themes and a great variety of related young adult fiction, picture books, and nonfiction titles.

Professional Discussion Questions

1. How can we get everyone involved in interdisciplinary units based on literature?

2. What themes appear in our current curriculum?

3. What literature titles would be appropriate?

4. Which current titles can we incorporate in our literature classes along with the classics?

5. What kinds of literature-based activities can we use?

Practical Application

Samples of Literature Themes

Holocaust—Picture Books

Adler, David A. *A Picture Book of Anne Frank.* Holiday House, 1993.

———. *Hiding from the Nazis.* Holiday House, 1997.

Hoestlandt, Jo. *Star of Fear, Star of Hope.* Walker, 1995.

Innocenti, Roberto. *Rose Blanche.* Creative Education, 1985.

Mochizuki, Ken. *Passage to Freedom: The Sugihara Story.* Lee & Low, 1997.

Sonderling, Eric. *A Knock at the Door.* Raintree Steck-Vaughn, 1997.

Wild, Margaret. *Let the Celebrations Begin.* Orchard Books, 1991.

Holocaust—Young Adult

Adler, David A. *We Remember the Holocaust.* Holt Paper, 1995.

Drucker, Malka, and Michael Halperin. *Jacob's Rescue.* Bantam Books, 1993.

Gold, Alison L. *Memories of Anne Frank: Reflections of a Childhood Friend.* Scholastic Incorporated, 1997.

Hurwitz, Johanna. *Anne Frank: Life in Hiding.* Jewish Publication Society, 1989.

Levitin, Sonia. *Journey to America.* Macmillan Publishing Company, 1970.

Lobel, Anita. *No Pretty Pictures.* Greenwillow Books, 1998.

Lowry, Lois. *Number the Stars.* Houghton Mifflin Company, 1989.

Napoli, Donna Jo. *Stones in Water.* Scholastic Incorporated, 1997.

Opdyke, Irene Cut. *In My Hands: Memories of a Holocaust Rescuer.* Alfred A. Knopf, 1999.

Reuter, Bjarne. *The Boys from St. Petri.* Puffin Books, 1991.

Schnur, Steven. *The Shadow Children.* Morrow Junior Books, 1994.

Williams, Laura E. *Behind the Bedroom Wall.* Milkweed, 1996.

Van der Rol, Ruud, and Rian Verhoeven. *Anne Frank: Beyond the Diary.* Viking Press, 1993.

Vos, Ida. *Anna Is Still Here.* Houghton Mifflin Company, 1993.

Yolen, Jane. *The Devil's Arithmetic.* Puffin Paper, 1988.

Civil War—Picture Books

Bunting, Eve. *The Blue and the Gray.* Scholastic Incorporated, 1996.

Polocco, Patricia. *Pink and Say.* Philomel, 1994.

Civil War—Young Adult

Beatty, Patricia. *Who Comes with Cannons?* Morrow Junior Books, 1992.

Donohue, John. *An Island Far from Home.* Carolrhoda, 1994.

Fleischman, Paul. *Bull Run.* HarperCollins, 1993.

Freedman, Russell. *Lincoln: A Photobiography.* Houghton Mifflin Company, 1987.

Hoobler, Thomas, and Dorothy Hoobler. *Sally Bradford: The Story of a Rebel Girl.* Silver Burdett, 1997.

Hunt, Irene. *Across Five Aprils.* Silver Burdett Paper, 1993.

Lincoln, Abraham. *The Gettysburg Address.* Houghton Mifflin Company, 1995.

Paulsen Gary. *Soldier's Heart.* Delacorte Press, 1998.

Reeder, Carolyn. *Shades of Gray.* Avon Books, 1989.

Reit, Seymour. *Behind the Rebel Lines.* Harcout Brace & Company, 1988.

Rinaldi, Ann. *Amelia's War.* Scholastic Press, 1999.

Shura, Mary Francis. *Gentle Annie: The True Story of a Civil War Nurse.* Scholastic Incorporated, 1991.

Stevens, Bryna. *Frank Thompson: Her Civil War Story.* Macmillan Publishing Company, 1992.

Wisler, G. Clifton. *Thunder on the Tennessee.* Puffin Books, 1983.

———. *Red Cap.* Puffin Books, 1991.

———. *Mr. Lincoln's Drummer.* Scholastic Incorporated, 1995.

Ecology—Picture Books

Cherry, Lynne. *The Great Kapok Tree: A Tale of the Amazon Rain Forest.* Harcourt Brace and Company, 1990.

Locker, Thomas. *The Land of Gray Wolf.* Dial Books for Young Readers, 1991.

MacGill-Callahan, Sheila. *And Still the Turtle Watched.* Dial Books for Young Readers, 1991.

Van Allsburg, Chris. *Just a Dream.* Houghton Mifflin Company, 1990.

Yolen, Jane. *Letting Swift River Go.* Little, Brown, 1992.

Ecology—Young Adult

Abelove, Joan. *Go and Come Back.* DK Publishing, 1998.

Anastasio, Dina. *The Case of the Glacier Park Swallow.* Roberts Rinehart Paper, 1994.

DeFelice, Cynthia. *Weasel.* Simon and Schuster, 1991.

———. *Lostman's River.* Macmillan Paper, 1994.

George, Jean Craighead. *The Talking Earth.* HarperTrophy, 1983.

———. *The Missing 'Gator of Gumbo Limbo.* HarperCollins, 1992.

———. *The Fire Bug Connection.* HarperCollins, 1993.

Smith, Roland. *Thunder Cave.* Hyperion Books for Children, 1995.

———. *Jaguar.* Hyperion Paperbacks for Children, 1997.

Math—Picture Books

Burns, Marilyn. *Spaghetti and Meatballs for All! A Mathematical Story.* Scholastic Incorporated, 1997.

Demi, *One Grain of Rice: A Mathematical Folktale.* Henry Holt, 1997.

Lasky, Kathryn. *The Librarian Who Measured the Earth.* Little, Brown and Company, 1994.

Neuschwander, Cindy. *Sir Cumference and the First Round Table: A Math Adventure.* Charlesbridge Publishing, 1997.

———. *Sir Cumference and the Dragon of Pi: A Math Adventure.* Charlesbridge Publishing, 1999.

Scieszka, Jon. *Math Curse.* Penguin, 1995.

Math—Young Adult

Enzensberger, Hans Magnus. *The Number Devil: A Mathematical Adventure.* Henry Holt and Company, 1997.

Ancient Egypt—Picture Books

Aliki. *Mummies Made in Egypt.* HarperCollins, 1979.

Climo, Shirley. *The Egyptian Cinderella.* HarperCollins Children's Book Group, 1992.

Mike, Jan. *Gift of the Nile: An Egyptian Legend.* Troll Associates, 1993.

Sabuda, Robert. *Tutankhamen's Gift.* Aladdin Paperbacks, 1994.

Ancient Egypt—Young Adult

Carter, Dorothy. *His Majesty, Queen Hatshepsut.* Lippincott Williams & Wilkins Publishers, 1987.

Levithan, David. *The Mummy.* Scholastic Incorporated, 1999.

Snyder, Zilpha Keatley. *The Egypt Game.* Yearling Books, 1967.

Annotated Professional Journal Articles

Allen, Susan, and Deborah Regan Howe. "A Novel Approach: A Teacher-Librarian Collaboration Brings Young Adult Literature into the Classroom," *VOYA* (December 1999): 314-17.

Reading may be a solitary activity, but the strong emotions created by young adult fiction need to be shared. This article shares a middle school curriculum-related themed booklist created by an English teacher and a librarian. Multiple copies of each book are available. The discussion focuses on grasping the bigger picture—identifying themes and comparing and contrasting diverse experiences. The teacher booktalks each book on the list, and the students read several from the list. The article topic is "immigrants" and is subdivided into shorter lists by time periods, beginning with 1620 and ending with present day. There is an annotation for each book and ordering information.

Cook, G., and M. Martinello. "Topics and Themes in Interdisciplinary Curriculum," *Middle School Journal* (January 1994): 40-44.

The article says that teachers use varied approaches to develop theme studies so that they are well integrated with regular curriculum guidelines. Themes are large ideas that integrate the concepts of several different disciplines. There are several criteria that help determine if a theme is important enough to warrant study. Is the big idea true over space and time? Does it broaden students' understanding of the world? Is the big idea interdisciplinary? Does it relate to students' genuine interest? Does it lead to student inquiry? Themes should be drawn from students' common interests, and they should encourage students to explore their own questions. They should go far beyond the limitations of textbooks, which should only serve as a starting point or for reference. Students should be encouraged to use a wide variety of resources.

Isaacs, Kathleen. "Classroom Connections: U.S. Geography in Fiction," *Book Links* (July 2000): 8-12.

A list of stories with literary qualities that allow the reader to understand the climate and culture of different areas of the United States is provided. These books are not meant to teach geography but to provide insight into the earth's complexities, different experiences and cultures, physical and human characteristics, and a sense of place. The books are grouped by regions of the United States and are for middle school readers.

Loftis, Susanna Sian. "Beyond Boundaries: Change Happens," *Book Links* (May 1999): 52-56.

Book Links is a fantastic resource for themed booklists. Every issue has several, and often they are geared to middle grades and older. All entries have ordering information and annotations. This theme is change and focuses on the middle school student who wants to be independent and mature, but who still welcomes the ties that bind. Change can be both welcomed and feared. Feelings of confusion, insecurity, anger, and loss abound as adolescents grow. Books provide a safe common ground for discussion about change. Students begin to realize the importance of a good book, and sharing feelings helps them realize they are not alone.

Moreillon, Judi. "Beyond Boundaries: Stories within Stories," *Book Links* (May 2000): 10-13.

Many titles can be shared in a culturally diverse classroom to help students understand one another and to increase their knowledge of the world, as well as to help build community among classmates. All of these titles contain key characters who are storytellers and who share information and insight about life. The list of titles includes picture books and fiction for all ages.

Segal, Marta. "Beyond Boundaries: Student-Teacher Relationships," *Book Links* (September 1999): 22-26.

The books in this themed list are about teachers and students, with subject matter that can be applied to different topics and content areas. All are about issues that concern kids and issues that you may want them to discuss. These books will not cure communication problems; they won't prevent things from happening, but they may prompt honest conversations and provide a good starting point for opening the lines of communication.

Smith, J., and Holly Johnson. "Bring It Together: Literature in an Integrative Curriculum," *Middle School Journal* (September 1993): 3-7.

This article discusses the integrative curriculum approach and uses literature to examine a theme. It combines concerns of adolescents and world issues rather than concentrating on fragmented, traditional subjects with content textbooks. Narratives are used as primary reading materials as are nonfiction books. The article provides information on teachers working together in teams to make the most of integration. It also lists five stages of developing integrated units: identify the thematic focus; select the narrative text; brainstorm and choose study objectives; develop instructional lessons and activities; establish an evaluation criteria, and plan the logistics. The article also includes some examples of novels and possible themes.

Wood, K., J. Flood, and D. Lapp. "Linking the Disciplines through Literature," *Middle School Journal* (November 1994): 65-67.

Good literature can be used across the curriculum to make the learning of subject matter more meaningful, universal, and cohesive. Integrating the curriculum means deliberately pointing out the connections between subjects rather than assuming that the students will automatically make these connections. The article suggests focusing on themes or topics and provides a historical perspective for the concept of integrated curriculum. The rest of the article focuses on an example of an integrated unit using *The Giver* by Lois Lowry. The activities are organized in centers, and they include having students: create their own version of utopia, read other science fiction with similar themes, find current events that parallel the occurrences in the story, compare the book with the Arizona Biosphere experiment, and create a time capsule.

Annotated Professional Books

Adamson, Lynda. *Literature Connections to World History Grades 7-12*. Libraries Unlimited, 1998.

Literature Connections is organized by historical topics and lists of titles. The topics include prehistory, Roman Empire, Europe and the British Isles, all the Asian countries, South Africa, Australia, Pacific Islands, and so on. There is an annotated bibliography of all titles at the end of the book. An annotated bibliography of CDs and videos is also provided.

Beers, Kylene, and Barbara Samuels, eds. *Into Focus: Understanding and Creating Middle School Readers*. Christopher-Gordon, 1998.

There are 22 essays in this volume written by 27 authors on a wide variety of topics of interest to those working with middle school students. The topics include understanding middle school students, choosing not to read, gifted middle school readers, struggling readers, reader response theory, thematic units and readers workshop, literature discussions, literature circles, journals, content area reading, authentic reading assessment, short stories, novels, and reading on the Internet.

Berman, Matt. *What Else Should I Read? Guiding Kids to Good Books*. Libraries Unlimited, 1996.

As librarians and teachers, we have all been asked, "Is there another book just like this?" Berman includes 30 book webs that highlight eight topics pertinent to the main title. Then each topic has several additional annotated books displayed in the form of a bookmark. This book is meant to be copied with its book web posted on a bulletin board and the bookmarks placed in the pocket of a book. Only fiction books are included, and it is a good source for students who are looking for something else to read.

Booth, David, ed. *Literacy Techniques for Building Successful Readers and Writers*. Pembroke, 1996.

This is a comprehensive handbook for teaching reading and writing—a collection of strategies and an overview of 100 major approaches to encourage literacy. Each strategy includes a brief discussion of the issues and then focuses on ready-to-use ideas for the classroom. Topics include assessment, literature circles, thematic units, journals, vocabulary, peer tutors, mini-lessons, and much more.

Chatton, B., and N. L. Collins. *Blurring the Edges: Integrated Curriculum through Writing and Children's Literature*. Heinemann, 1999.

The authors provide possibilities for combining subjects, themes, and genres. The index at the back of the book is divided by authors, titles, and subjects. The chapters deal with the writing process and reading and writing across the curriculum. There are thematic units on mystery, magic and history; letters and diaries; math, science, and textures. Each section has annotated lists of children's books that provide information and support children's studies.

Ellis, A. K., and C. Stuen. *The Interdisciplinary Curriculum*. Eye on Education, 1998.

The introduction discusses the knowledge explosion, curriculum coverage, and fragmented learning. The first chapter contains a research base for the interdisciplinary curriculum and an agenda for the future. Different approaches to an interdisciplinary curriculum are explored, including the project, discovery, and theme. There is information on team teaching and cooperative learning. The book concludes with a variety of sample units and a list of resources.

Herz, S. *From Hinton to Hamlet: Building Bridges between Young Adult Literature and the Classics*. Greenwood Press, 1996.

The value of young adult literature lies in its ability to draw students' attention into the story immediately because it deals with real problems in their own lives. Young adult literature gives students the right to experience reading as a pleasurable activity and helps them to become competent readers. The following are unique characteristics of young adult literature: the main character is a teenager; the events, problems, and plots are related to teens; the dialogue reflects teenage speech; the point of view is from an adolescent's perspective; the novel is short; and the actions and decisions of the main characters are major factors in the outcome of the conflict. It is suggested that young adult literature should be an important part of literature classes because it can be used as a bridge to the classics.

Hurst, Carol Otis, and Rebecca Otis. *Using Literature in the Middle School Curriculum*. Linworth, 1999.

This title begins with a cross-reference chart listing all themes and focus books and indicating possible content areas (science, history, sociology, art, music, physical education, and mathematics) for integration. The authors share information on classroom techniques, including crossing disciplines, group discussions, literature groups, and sample mini-lessons. Next there are 18 chapters of themes and topics: slavery, going West, Native Americans, the Holocaust, immigration, protests and rebellions, biography, survival, picture books, sports, humor, and so forth. There is a section on literary study covering foreshadowing, climax, symbolism, allegories, flashbacks, points of view, and cliffhangers. The last section features 29 chapters, each about an individual focus book. Each chapter discusses the plot, and taking it deeper, and includes a list of related books.

Hurst, Carol Otis, Lynn Otis Palmer, Vaughn Churchill, Margaret Sullivan Ahern, and Bernard G. McMahon. *Curriculum Connections: Picture Books in Grade 3 and Up*. Linworth, 1999.

Eighty-five picture books are covered, with possible themes and curriculum ties and the strongest curriculum areas represented in each book. There is a lesson on each title, which includes a summary; illustration information; novel, theme, and curriculum connections; lessons in all curriculum areas; and a long annotated list of related books.

International Society for Technology in Education. *National Educational Technology Standards for Students.* ISTE, 2000.

A discussion about connecting curriculum and technology includes essential conditions, the definition of curriculum integration, and information on how to use the book and beyond. The second section lists the technology standards for PK through 2, 3 through 5, 6 through 8, and 9 through 12 and includes profiles, performance indicators, curriculum examples, and scenarios. The third section contains specific examples of curriculum integration for all grade levels in these areas: language arts, foreign language, math, science, and social studies. The fourth section includes multidisciplinary resource units for all grade levels. There are also very complete appendixes with many resources for teachers and technology coordinators.

Langer, Judith. *Envisioning Literature: Literary Understanding and Literature Instruction.* Teachers College Press, 1995.

Interacting with texts, literary discussions, strategies for teaching, literature for students the system has failed, literary concepts and vocabulary, and literature across the curriculum are some of the topics discussed in this book about literature for middle and high school students.

McElmeel, Sharron. *Great New Nonfiction Reads.* Libraries Unlimited, 1995.

To determine an information book's potential appeal one needs to consider the attractiveness of the cover, the credibility of the author, the copyright date, whether the book gives accurate information on all sides of the topic, the accuracy of the graphics, and the book's organization. This book encourages the reading of nonfiction books aloud, and ways to respond. It even includes 25 ideas for general responses. The majority of the book lists nonfiction titles, some annotated, by topics.

Moss, Joy. *Using Literature in the Middle Grades: A Thematic Approach.* Christopher-Gordon, 1994.

The introductory chapter gives valuable background information on developing a literature program with thematic units. It includes basic assumptions, reading literature with students, questioning, reading-writing connection, sharing literary experiences, collaboration, and step-by-step instructions for developing focus units. There is also a very useful appendix listing resources for teachers.

Moss, Joy. *Teaching Literature in the Middle Grades: A Thematic Approach.* Christopher-Gordon, 2000.

A focus unit begins with a general discussion of literature in the middle grade classroom. The author refers to Rosenblatt's transactional theory of reading, in which the reader becomes part of the story and shares the experiences. The remaining chapters are focus units on friendship, modern fairy tales, dilemmas and decisions, family, artists, war and peace, on their own, between two worlds, and Cinderella variants. Each unit gives a list of appropriate titles, library journal and dialogue group ideas, detailed shared reading experiences, reading and writing connections, and synthesis and assessment suggestions.

Roberts, Patricia, and Richard Kellough. *A Guide for Developing Interdisciplinary Thematic Units.* Prentice-Hall/Merrill, 2000.

The introduction to an interdisciplinary thematic unit includes knowledge and meaningful learning; multilevel instruction; integrated curriculum purposes; the role of teacher, school, and modern technology; as well as summary questions. Next, directions are given on selecting a theme, aligning it with standards, developing a scope and sequence, developing objectives, learning activities, assessments, and lesson planning. The book also includes sample units. It is a great source of information for getting started in planning these units.

Sheppard, Ronnie, and Beverly Stratton. *Reflections on Becoming: Fifteen Literature-Based Units for the Young Adolescent.* National Middle School Association, 1993.

Insights on early adolescent literature and 15 units based on novels comprise this book. It concludes with directions and suggestions for the professional to prepare similar units on other novels.

Web Sites

Book Links Magazine
   http://www.ala.org/BookLinks/

Classroom Connect—Ideas for Projects
   http://www.classroomconnect.com/

Clearinghouse for Math and Science Ideas and Projects
   http://www.enc.org/

Electronic Emissary—Projects and Mentors
   http://emissary.ots.utexas.edu/emissary/index.html

Global Schoolhouse Collaborative Projects
   http://www.gsh.org/

Middle School Projects (technology integration)
   http://www.ecb.org/ttt/middle.htm

Projects and Resources
   http://www.teachnet.org/

10
Current
Young Adult Literature

Too often young adults are being forced to read classics in their literature classes. Many teachers do not feel that current young adult literature is written well enough to be included in the literature curriculum. More often than not, literature teachers teach a classic to death and then tell their colleagues that the students really enjoyed the book. These teachers are not providing literature that makes a connection for their students. In order to foster a lifelong love of reading, teachers have to provide time for reading in class and let students choose from a large selection of current young adult titles.

Herz (1996), in *From Hinton to Hamlet: Building Bridges between Young Adult Literature and the Classics,* states that the value of young adult literature lies in its ability to draw students' attention into the story immediately by dealing with real problems in their own lives and eliminating social barriers. Herz feels that all adolescent students should be given the right to experience reading as a pleasurable activity.

There are certain characteristics that are common to all young adult literature: the main character is a teenager; the events and problems in the plot are related to teenagers; the main character is the center of the plot; the dialogue reflects teenage speech, including slang; the point of view presents an adolescent's interpretation of events and people; the teenage main character is usually perceptive, sensitive, intelligent, mature, and independent; the novel is short, rarely more than 200 pages; and the actions and decisions of the main characters are major factors in the outcome of the conflict.

Herz claims that YA is "anything that readers anywhere between the approximate ages of twelve and twenty choose to read—as opposed to what they may be coerced to read for class assignments." YA is typecast by many teachers as being inferior reading and lacking the necessary qualities of great works of literature. Yet it has been proven to be an effective means to motivate adolescents to read all kinds of literature, including the classics. She feels that teachers should get away from study questions and the teacher's correct interpretation of the novel, in order to assist, help, force, and convince our students to appreciate "good" literature.

Transaction between reader and text first happens when the reader constructs meaning from the novel. Each reader uses personal experiences as a bridge to meaning. Next, it is social—when readers want to share their reactions to books. The more they read, the more readers begin to recognize patterns: settings, characters, plots, and so forth. Change from teacher-centered class to student-centered response-based class, and help the readers make connections, build bridges, and really enjoy their choice of YA titles.

Fine (1996) points out that magazines are extremely popular reading material for adolescents, and that libraries should include a good selection of the most popular periodicals. Also, webzines are becoming more numerous and are easily accessed on the Internet.

The Michael L. Printz Award exemplifies the best in current young adult literature. This new award, along with its honor books, now recognizes current YA titles on the same level as the Newbery and Caldecott awards, and also provides the same publicity.

Bruggeman (1997) encourages librarians to include the latest in high-quality graphic novels in their adolescent collections.

Kist (2000) advises that the new literacy include script writing, film production, graphic arts, and multimedia.

According to Carter (2000), author Chris Crutcher, winner of the Edwards Award, doesn't flinch from writing about the most difficult subjects. His stories give hope to young people as they struggle to find out who they are and where they belong. This bold approach is becoming more and more popular with young adult authors.

Sullivan (1998) points out how important cover art is for adolescents. Often that is how they make selections, and Sullivan feels that publishers of young adult fiction should collaborate with adolescent students when making their cover-art selections.

Barrett (2000) encourages teachers of adolescents to read aloud in all content area classes—not just in literature classes. Reading aloud develops vocabulary, makes students aware of the author's style and meaning, stimulates language growth, encourages dialogue, and introduces students to books and authors they might not select on their own.

Decker (2000) reviews young adult titles for emerging teen readers who are searching for appealing plots, strong characters, and mature subject matter without sensationalism or profanity.

The Michael L. Printz Award for Excellence in Young Adult Literature was first presented in 2000. This award is sponsored by *Booklist*, a publication of the American Library Association. It is named for a Topeka, Kansas, school librarian who was a longtime active member of TheYoung Adult Library Services Association. This is a very important award for young adult literature—it finally gives some credibility to the genre.

◂◂ 2000 Award Winner

Myers, Walter Dean. *Monster*. HarperCollins Children's Book Group, 1999.

◂◂ 2000 Honor Books

Almond, David. *Skellig*. Delacorte Press, 1999.

Halse, Laurie. *Speak*. Farrar Straus and Giroux, 1999.

Wittlinger, Ellen. *Hard Love*. Simon & Schuster Books for Young Readers, 1999.

Professional Discussion Questions

1. Do we include current young adult titles in our literature classes?

2. Do we have a wide selection of current young adult titles in our library?

3. Do we allow students to participate in the selection of titles for the library?

4. Do we give our students time to read young adult novels?

5. Do we give our students time to discuss their feeling about their reading?

Annotated Current Young Adult Literature

Bauer, Joan. *Backwater*. Putnam Publishing Goup, 1999.

Ivy Breedlove, 16, plans to be a historian. She has 63 days to finish researching the Breedlove family in time for Great Aunt Tib's 80th birthday. "People think it's exciting being part of a family with so many successful lawyers. I tell them it's like being a goldfish swimming in a tank stocked with snapping turtles—it's hard to keep a lasting presence."

At family gatherings, Ivy is said to be like her Aunt Josephine, and "being like Josephine was not a compliment." Aunt Josephine is a sculptor and recluse whose whereabouts are unknown. Ivy desires to find her Aunt, interview her, and complete her family history. Ivy overcomes many hardships and finds her Aunt along with a missing piece of herself in the process.

Billingsley, Franny. *The Folk Keeper*. Atheneum Books for Young Readers, 1999.

Written in the form of a journal, this is the story of Corinna Stonewall, an orphan from a foundling home, who disguises herself as a boy so that she can become a folk keeper. She is never cold, she always knows what time it is, and her hair grows two inches while she sleeps. She is called by Lord Merton to come to his seaside estate, Cliffsend, in the Northern Isles, to be the folk keeper. She discovers that he is her father and eventually finds out who her mother was. She takes the job and prides herself on her skills of feeding, distracting, and pacifying the furious, ravenous folk at Cliffsend. She meets someone and falls in love, but in the end she must decide where she really belongs.

Block, Francesca Lia. *Violet & Claire*. HarperCollins Publishers, 1999.

Violet comes from a well-to-do family and is an avid writer working on a screenplay. Her peers shun her because of her strange dress and attitude. She is looking for a star for her screenplay and discovers Claire. They begin an unusual friendship. Violet's screenplay is sold for a six-figure sum, and Claire and Violet become involved with the same man.

Cart, Michael, comp. *Tomorrowland: Ten Stories about the Future*. Scholastic Press, 1999.

Michael Cart, author and former director of the Beverly Hills Public Library, has compiled these short stories from famous young adult authors such as Jon Sciesszka, Rodman Philbrick, Lois Lowry, Tor Seidler, Gloria Skurzynski, Ron Koertge, Katherine Paterson, Jacqueline Woodson, and James Cross Giblin. The stories vary in their approach to tomorrowland. Several of the authors look to the past and see what the ancients imagined the future to be. Some of the authors select the present day, and others reach out to a time here-tofore. One particularly disturbing story is "The Last Book in the Universe" by Rodman Phil-brick. His story answers the questions: "What if there came a time when no one read books? What if books and the whole concept of reading had been forgotten? What would the world be like? What would the people be like?" At the end of each story, the author tells what prompted him or her to write the story in the Author's Note. At the conclusion of many of the stories the reader may not want them to end—and maybe they are actually just beginning.

Cormier, Robert. *Frenchtown Summer*. Delacorte Press, 1999.

Done in verse, this is the story of a young boy's life in an ethnic neighborhood long ago. He shares his feelings about his parents, his immediate family, and extended family and friends. All senses are addressed as the boy describes his emotions and activities during this remembered summer.

Farmer, Nancy. *A Girl Named Disaster*. Puffin Books, 1996.

Nhamo is being raised by her mother's family. Since this is traditionally not the cus-tom, she is made to do all the manual work. Ambuya, or Grandmother, is the only one who is kind to Nhamo. Nhamo's mother was killed by a leopard, and her father was a murderer. Ac-cording to Muvuki the angry spirit of the murdered man demanded that Nhamo marry a dis-eased man with several wives. Ambuya shares a plan with Nhamo and tells her to take what she needs to survive and leave the village. Nhamo takes the only canoe and travels from Mozambique to Zimbabwe, where her father's family lives. Her journey is full of perils and dangers, but she is helped along the way by mystical spirits.

Fletcher, Ralph. *Fig Pudding*. Houghton Mifflin Company, 1995.

The Abernathy family has six kids. The oldest boy tells the story of how he is often left to care for them all—except the youngest one—and then the parents blame him when things get crazy. The normal family life becomes greatly disrupted when one of the boys dies from injuries sustained while bike riding. The family struggles to deal with the loss.

Gee, Maurice. *The Fat Man*. Simon & Schuster Children's Publishing, 1997.

Colin has a chance encounter with a fat man at the creek, and a long time later the man comes to live in Loomis. Colin learns he is Herbert Muskie, and that he has come back to town for revenge on everyone there who made fun of him as a child.

Gutman, Dan. *Honus & Me*. Avon Books, 1997.

Joe has just struck out again. He loves the game of baseball, but he is not very good at it. Money is scarce at home, and his mother arranges for Joe to clean out the attic of their neighbor, elderly Amanda Young. Most of the attic was clean except for one box, which falls apart when he picks it up. Upon closer inspection, Joe finds a rare T-206 Honus Wagner baseball card. This card is valuable because it is worth a-half million dollars, and also be-cause it allows Honus Wagner to travel forward in time and Joe to travel back in time with Honus. Through unusual circumstances, Joe plays in the 1909 World Series and has a key hit to help the Pirates win. Joe learns the secret to being a great ballplayer: trick yourself into thinking you already are.

Jordan, Sherryl. *The Raging Quiet.* Simon & Schuster Books for Young Readers, 1999.

Marne was unafraid of work and attracted the attention of the Lord's middle son, Isake. When her father suffered a stroke and was unable to work, Marne agreed to marry Isake so that her family could remain in the overseer's house. Isake and Marne relocate to the fishing hamlet of Torcurra. Two days later, Isake falls to his death from the roof of their little cottage. Marne befriends a youth whom everyone thinks is a madman. Marne learns that he is not mad but deaf. She develops a sign language so that they are able to communicate. The local townspeople are suspicious of anyone who is different. Gradually, they believe that Marne is a witch who put a curse on her late husband and converses with Raven, the madman. They put her on trial as a witch. How will she be able to survive the trials ahead? "This tale belongs to any time, even our own; it is about prejudice and ignorance, and a young woman wrongly accused, who is guilty of only one thing—the unforgivable crime of being different."

LaFaye, A. *The Year of the Sawdust Man.* Simon & Schuster Books for Young Readers, 1998.

Eleven-year-old Nissa lives in the small town of Harper, Louisiana. The local townswomen do not like her outspoken, freedom-loving, nonconventional mother, Heirah, and frequently gossip about her. Nissa arrives home one day from school and finds that all of her mother's purple roses have been cut. Nissa knows immediately that her mother has left for good. Nissa feels abandoned no matter what her father says. When Papa begins to date, and in time marry Miss Lara Ross, Nissa doesn't know how she will cope with Lara as her day-to-day mama. Nissa is a lot like her mother in all of the good ways—creative, loving, spirited, and honest. In time, Mama does come back into Nissa's life, and Nissa feels as if she has it all, including Lara.

Metzger, Lois. *Missing Girls.* Viking Press, 1999.

Carrie was sent to live with her grandmother for one year while her father worked in another state. Her mother died four years ago, and Carrie has been in a dream state ever since. She meets Mona, whose home life looks ideal to the casual observer. In time, Carrie sees the darkness in the modern lightness of Mona's home, and the light in the darkness of her home with Grandmother. She decides that she no longer wants to sleep away the rest of her life.

Myers, Walter Dean. *Monster.* HarperCollins Children's Book Group, 1999.

Steven Harmon, 16, is on trial for murder. He is witnessing and scripting his own trial as if he were producing a movie. Throughout this unusual format one has a sense of how and why this murder was committed and the pressures these young men endure both in and out of prison. At one point Steve asks, "You think we're going to win?" His attorney responds, "It probably depends on what you mean by 'win'." There are no winners in this thought-provoking novel.

Nix, Garth. *Shade's Children.* HarperCollins Children's Book Group, 1997.

This is a dark story of a post-nuclear-war world ruled by Overlords who take children's brains and bodies to create monsters who fight for their masters. Shade is not really human but a holographic image coming from a computer. Shade provides food and shelter in an abandoned submarine for children who try to get information about the Overlords. Finally, the children set out to try on their own to destroy the Overlords.

Nixon, Joan Lowry. *Search for the Shadowman.* Delacorte Press, 1996.

Was Joe Cooley a thief? Did he steal the family homestead money and set off for the western states? Who is threatening Andy to stop his research about Joe?

It all begins when Andy is assigned to research his family history and produce a report about earlier life and times. When Andy tries to interview his great Aunt Minnie, she will not discuss Joe Cooley. It was thought that Joe ran off with the family money and thereafter was a disgrace. Andy sets out to prove otherwise. He learns what really happened to Joe, but if he reveals the complete truth he will lose his best friend.

Nolan, Han. *Dancing on the Edge.* Harcourt Brace, 1997.

Miracle McCloy was named Miracle by her grandmother, Gigi, because she was born "out of the body of a dead woman." Sissy, Miracle's mother, was in an accident with an ambulance and was killed. Miracle lives with Dane, her father, and Gigi, who practices the occult and communicates with spirits. Dane was a child prodigy and wrote his first book at a young age. When Sissy died at 17, Dane never wrote another book and became a recluse in the McCloy home.

When Miracle is about 12, Gigi teaches her to become an apprentice. On the night of Miracle's first séance, Sissy communicates through a Ouija board. "Dane's gone, N-O-W." Gigi explains Dane's strange disappearance: he's melted. From that moment on, Miracle tries to bring Dane back. Miracle's actions become bizarre as her surroundings frighten her and bring her closer to the edge. In a test to find out if she is real, Miracle sets herself on fire.

After her medical recovery, Aunt Casey arranges for Miracle's transfer to The Cedars. Dr. DeAngelis, a young psychiatrist, works with Miracle and her search for the truth and love that make her feel real. A powerful National Book Award winner.

Paterson, Katherine. *Preacher's Boy.* Clarion Books, 1999.

Robbie is 11 years old, and he is the son of a preacher. He is full of mischief, especially after he hears a sermon stating that the end of the world may be in six months, at the turn of the century. He decides to be an apeists (atheist) so he doesn't have to bother with the Ten Commandments. His one ambition is to ride in a motorcar before the world goes bust. Never mind the fact that he has only seen one motorcar in his life. How Robbie achieves his dream makes for a humorous and entertaining read.

Paulsen, Gary. *The Schernoff Discoveries.* Delacorte Press, 1997.

This story is told by the best friend of Harold Schernoff, a 14-year-old science whiz, nerd, and social outcast. The two stick together through thick and thin, and Harold is always making discoveries and getting them both into crazy situations.

Roberts, Willo Davis. *The Kidnappers: A Mystery.* Atheneum Books for Young Readers, 1998.

Joey Bishop has a vivid imagination and can really tell stories. Then when he sees a classmate being kidnapped, no one believes him. He finally gets his father to call the police; then he is taken more seriously when further scary things start happening.

Sachar, Louis. *Holes*. Farrar Straus and Giroux, 1998.

Stanley Yelnats IV's, great-grandfather lost his entire fortune, and a curse is placed on his descendants. Our Stanley continues to have bad luck. He is sent to Camp Green Lake for a crime he didn't commit. Camp Green Lake is not at all what its name suggests: it is desolate and barren with no water in sight, so fences and guards are unnecessary. His punishment is to dig a hole 5 feet by 5 feet in width and depth every day in the hot sun before he is allowed to do anything else. Everything changes when Stanley finds a small gold tube with the initials K. B. This book won the Newbery Award in 1999.

Sleator, William. *The Boxes*. Dutton Children's Books, 1998.

Annie's uncle leaves her with two boxes. He tells her not to open them and to leave them separated—one in her closet and one in the basement. Fifteen-year-old Annie can't resist and opens the boxes. One contains telepathic creatures and the other a clock that stops time. At the same time, she and her aunt are being harassed by the unscrupulous Crutchly Development Company, which wants to purchase their home to make way for a new development.

Sones, Sonya. *Stop Pretending: What Happened When My Big Sister Went Crazy*. Harper-Collins, 1999.

An intimate, heartfelt portrayal of what it was like for the author when her older sister was hospitalized for a mental breakdown. This story is told through successive poems that express sorrow, bewilderment, loss, fears, loneliness, and happiness. The author shares her insights into the world of the mentally ill and its consequences on the family. In the author's note at the end of the short book, she tells you that her sister is now married and takes medicine to keep her disease under control. Phone numbers and web sites of mental health organizations are included. A powerful first book.

Williams, Laura E. *The Spider's Web*. Milkweed Editions, 1999.

Lexi is a neo-Nazi skinhead. She has just spray painted the local synagogue and is hiding on the porch of a nearby house. An elderly woman, Ursula, comes to the door and invites Lexi in after Lexi tells her that she is being followed. The hood of Lexi's sweatshirt comes loose and exposes her shaved head with the tattoo of a blue-black swastika like a spider above her ear. The sight of the tattoo triggers flashbacks for Ursula to the time when she was a member of Hitler Youth. Both Ursula and Lexi must take responsibility for their actions, one in the past and the other in the present.

Woodson, Jacqueline. *If You Come Softly*. Puffin Books, 1998.

Elisha, or Ellie, is in the ninth grade at Percy High School, a private school. She bumps into Jeremiah, or Miah, that very first day and immediately feels there is something familiar about him. Ellie is Jewish and Miah is black, and their first pure love is strained by the attitudes of strangers. They are both afraid of the racist attitudes of friends and family, and just as Ellie is ready to introduce Miah to her family, tradegy strikes.

The first time they are alone Miah quotes a poem his mother used to read to him, thus the title of the book.

Wynne-Jones, Tim. *Stephen Fair*. DK Publishing, 1998.

Stephen is suffering from nightmares—a baby crying, fires, a tree house. His older brother, Marcus, had had similar dreams and had left four years ago, right after their father left. Stephen's mother is terribly worried about him. She wants him to call her Brenda, not Mom. Stephen, at fifteen, is trying to discover what is going on in his family, why his mother was always upset, and why these dreams continue. He makes amazing discoveries.

Wynne-Jones, Tim. *Lord of the Fries and Other Stories*. DK Publishing, 1999.

This is a collection of stories about students who interact with classmates, teachers, and community characters in a light hearted and funny way.

Young, Karen Romano. *The Beetle and Me: A Love Story*. William Morrow and Company, 1999.

Daisy Pandolfi, a high school sophomore, is working on restoring the engine of a 1957 Volkswagen Beetle. She meets Billy Hatcher in auto-shop class, and she also works with him in the stage crew for the school musical. She has a disaster with the engine and struggles to fix it without help. She learns something important from Billy Hatcher in the process.

Annotated Professional Journal Articles

Barrett, Virginia Denise. "Are We Reading to Our Teens?" *Book Report* (May/June 2000): 35-38.

The author states that it is very important to read to teens. She says that sometimes literature teachers read aloud because they feel it is part of their subject, but content area teachers rarely read aloud. She lists benefits of reading aloud: building social relationships, teaching skills and conventions of language, improving comprehension, developing creative thinking and imagination, enhancing curriculum, improving listening and speaking skills, and motivating students to read. She also lists reading-aloud tips and many suggestions for making reading aloud part of your teaching.

Bruggeman, L. " 'Zap! Whoosh! Kerplow!' Build High-Quality Graphic Novel Collections with Impact," *School Library Journal* (January 1997): 22-27.

Graphic novels have continuing plots and characters; they are not the comics you read in the newspapers. They have a broad appeal, and there are several resource books available to help librarians make wise purchases for their collections. Graphic novels are a form of visual literacy, and they work well with reluctant readers who feel comfortable with some text and lots of graphics.

Carter, Betty. "Eyes Wide Open," *School Library Journal* (June 2000): 42-45.

Betty Carter interviews author Chris Crutcher. He is a therapist and often gets his ideas from his clients. He feels that children are sheltered too much and often are not prepared for the real world. Crutcher writes about the darker side of life because that is reality for many of his clients. He feels that adults need to know what can happen to teens and what horrors they can face. Crutcher is frustrated when his books are challenged because he feels teens need to know what can go on and how to combat the things they may face as they grow up.

Charles, John, Shelley Mosley, and Ann Bouricius. "Romancing the YA Reader," *VOYA* (February 1999): 414-15.

Librarians are happy to recommend adult titles in science fiction, historical fiction, mysteries, and fantasy, but when it comes to romance titles, they are unsure.

This article gives the definition of romance fiction as "happily ever after" with relationship-driven plots. The authors state that romance fiction readers are very loyal to their favorite authors. Romance fiction empowers women; there are feisty heroines and good role models for young adults. There are a variety of subgenres in romance fiction. The article offers a very complete list of reference books for helping librarians to make the right recommendations to their older young adult readers who are searching for good romance fiction titles.

Decker, Charlotte. "Too Old for Beverly Cleary, Too Young for Danielle Steel," *Book Report* (May/June 2000): 18-21.

This article reviews books in several genres that are suitable for younger teens. These books have protagonists 14 years old or younger, a softer edge, and are designed for the emerging teen reader. The books received positive reviews and, have appealing plots, strong characters, and mature subject matter without profanity of sensationalism. The article covers 31 titles from three genres.

Fine, Jana. "Teen 'Zines: Magazines & Webzines for the Way Cool Set," *School Library Journal* (November 1996): 34-37.

Fine sent questionnaires regarding the popularity of magazines to public libraries and schools in 10 states. She asked for the three favorite magazines, the three most disliked magazines, what teens looked for in magazines, and what topics they would like to see covered in magazines. *Seventeen* was the most popular magazine. The article also mentions webzines as a new format for trends, tastes, and interests of teens on the Internet.

Kist, William. "Beginning to Create the New Literacy Classroom: What Does the New Literacy Look Like?" *Journal of Adolescent and Adult Literacy* (May 2000): 710-18.

In the new literacy classroom there is an onslaught of new communication tools. Technology is increasingly multimodal—encompassing print and graphic art, music, mathematics, drama, cinema, and so on. The five characteristics of the new literacy are ongoing, continuous usage of multiple forms of representation, explicit discussion of symbol usage, students engaged in ongoing dialogues as they think through problems and create products, a balance of individual and collaborative activities, and diversified expression and mutual respect.

MacRae, Cathi Dunn. "The Myth of the Bleak Young Adult Novel," *VOYA* (December 1998): 325-27.

This article is a critique of an article by Sara Mosle that appeared in *The New York Times Sunday Magazine* entitled "The Outlook's Bleak" (August 2, 1998: 34). Mosle complains that the topics for most young adult novels are very disturbing. MacRae feels that this gives parents and teachers the impression that young adult literature is evil and should be avoided. She believes this is wrong, because teachers need to be discussing young adult novels with teens, and teens need to be reading them for their truthfulness, timeliness, and inspiration. MacRae says that reading current young adult novels leads to discussion, a sense of community, and encouragement for teens living in these challenging times.

Ryan, Sara. "It's Hip to Be Square," *School Library Journal* (March 2000): 138-41.

A variety of ideas for creating library web sites for teens as well as school sites are included here. The first suggestion is, do not link to really obvious sites and popular search engines. Next, there should be links to sites that highlight book reviews written by teens, and several sites are listed. It is also suggested that there should be links to local universities, state education department scholarships, nonprofit organizations for possible community service, and crisis centers, shelters, and various help hot lines. The site should be updated regularly and maintained by teens.

Sullivan, Edward. "Judging Books by Their Covers: A Cover Art Experiment," *VOYA* (August 1998): 180-82.

The author discusses the reasons publishers spend so much time creating catchy book covers for their new titles. According to the author, young adults really do judge a book by its cover. For a long time librarians have been asking that publishers provide cover illustrations that are true to the content of the books. The author had 21 young adults aged 11 to 17 rate 15 books solely on their cover art. The students all agreed that cover art is extremely important, and many of them would miss excellent reads if the cover art was not appealing. The author suggests that publishers should work very closely with teens in creating cover art.

Annotated Professional Books

Ammon, Bette D., and Gale W. Sherman. *More Rip-Roaring Reads for Reluctant Teen Readers*. Libraries Unlimited, 1999.

If we expect nonreaders to read, then we must give them choices: fiction, nonfiction, adventure, mystery, and a variety of alternatives. The purpose of this book is to reach those nonreaders by matching them with 40 spellbinding books written by notable authors. Each of these books meets several criteria: recent publication date, relatively short book length, appealing format, eye-catching cover, high-interest level, meaningful subject matter, appropriate reading levels (middle school or high school), notable authors, and excellent writing. Each entry includes genre and themes, readability and interest levels, reviews, author information, plot summary, hints on introducing the book, booktalks, literature extensions, bookmarks with additional titles, and two indexes.

Herz, S. *From Hinton to Hamlet: Building Bridges between Young Adult Literature and the Classics*. Greenwood Press, 1996.

The value of young adult literature lies in its ability to draw students' attention into the story immediately. It deals with real problems in their own lives. Young adult literature gives students the right to experience reading as a pleasurable activity and helps them to become competent readers. Unique characteristics of young adult literature include the following: the main character is a teenager; the events, problems, and plots are related to teens; the dialogue reflects teenage speech; the point of view is from an adolescent's perspective; the novel is short; and the actions and decisions of the main characters are major factors in the outcome of the conflict. This book suggests that young adult literature should be an important part of all literature classes. YA literature is an important bridge to the classics.

Kaywell, Joan, ed. *Adolescent Literature as a Complement to the Classics, Volume 4.* Christopher-Gordon, 2000.

Classic titles are connected with current young adult literature. The premise is that classics will be easier to understand and perhaps better accepted by adolescents if there is a connection to current literature. The classics discussed are *Our Town, Oliver Twist, The Crucible, My Antonia, A Lesson Before Dying, The Call of the Wild, The Hunchback of Notre Dame, Henry IV, Pride and Prejudice, I Heard the Owl Call My Name, The Once and Future King, The Dark Is Rising* series, *Cyrano de Bergerac, The Tragedy of Dr. Faustus,* and *Antigone.*

Simmons, John, and Lawrence Baines. *Language Study in Middle School, High School, and Beyond: Views on Enhancing the Study of Language.* International Reading Association, 1998.

Ten chapters, each by different authors, discuss language study in the contemporary classroom, whole language, poetry, linguistics, sociolinguistics, reading and writing in the shadow of film and television, and the future of the written word.

Stoll, Donald, ed. *Magazines for Kids and Teens.* International Reading Association, 1997.

Jim Trelease writes the foreword, and Stoll provides ideas on how to use magazines effectively. There is a complete listing of current magazines with description, audience, cost, ordering addresses, and other useful information.

Wadham, Tim and Rachel. *Bringing Fantasy Alive for Children and Young Adults.* Linworth, 1999.

The authors start with an overview of fantasy, including traditional and contemporary, children's responses, barriers to appreciating fantasy, and its literary aspects. The next section deals with practical ways to share fantasy with children, including integrating it into the curriculum through booktalks, programs, and story times. There is also an Internet section with online fantasy resources, general literature sites, author sites, and listserv discussion groups. Selected author biographies and extensive annotated lists of titles are divided by picture books, chapter books, and grade level.

Whitfield, Jamie. *Getting Kids Hooked on Literature: A Hands-On Guide to Making Literature Exciting for Kids.* Prufrock Press, 1998.

This book is divided into four chapters: conversations, discussions, and debates; art, movies and music; games and simulations; and reports and research. In each chapter three or four novels/books are featured with a variety of reproducible activities and suggestions for use.

Web Sites

Avi
> http://www.avi-writer.com/

Award Winning Children's Literature
> http://www2.wcoil.com/~ellerbee/childlit.html

Betsy Byars
> http://www.betsybyars.com/

Caldecott Award Home Page
> http://www.ala.org/alsc/caldecott.html

Children's Literature & Language Arts Resources
> http://falcon.jmu.edu/~ramseyil/childlit.htm

Coretta Scott King Award Home Page
> http://www.ala.org/srrt/csking/

Gary Paulsen
> http://www.scils.rutgers.edu/special/kay/paulsen.html

Jean Craighead George
> http://www.jeancraigheadgeorge.com/

Judy Blume
> http://www.judyblume.com/

Katherine Paterson
> http://www.terabithia.com/

Kids Web Literature
> http://www.npac.syr.edu/textbook/kidsweb/Arts/literature.html

Learning to Read
> http://www.toread.com

Michael L. Printz Award
> http://www.ala.org/yalsa/printz/index.html

Newbery Award Home Page
> http://www.ala.org/alsc/newbery.html

Patricia Polacco's
> http://www.patriciapolacco.com/

Randolph Caldecott Society
> http://macserver.stjohns.k12.fl.us/others/rc.html

Sunshine State Young Reader's Award
> http://www.sdhc.k12.fl.us/mediaweb/SSYRA/ssyra.htm

11

Reading
in the Content Areas

Most content area teachers do not feel prepared to teach reading, nor do they want the responsibility for teaching reading—reading should have been taught in the upper elementary grades at the very latest. Content area texts can pose a serious problem for many young adult readers. They have no prior knowledge in many of the topic areas, and the text is difficult to read and comprehend. Experts in the field write the text, and the delivery is not necessarily user-friendly to young adults. Many students need to be taught a wide variety of strategies in order to cope.

Billmeyer and Barton (1998) state that teaching reading in the content areas is not so much about teaching students basic reading skills as it is about teaching students how to use reading as a tool for thinking and learning. Readers construct meaning as they read; effective readers are strategic, they make predictions, organize information, and interact with the text. They evaluate ideas in light of what they already know. They monitor comprehension and know how to modify their reading behaviors when they have problems understanding what they read.

Cognitive science identifies five premises that are basic to the teaching of content area reading skills:

1. The meaning of text is not contained in the words on the page; the reader constructs meaning by making a connection with the words on the page and what he or she already knows.

2. The single most important variable in learning with texts is a reader's prior knowledge.

3. How well a reader comprehends a text is also dependent on metacognition—the ability to think about and control the reading process before, during, and after reading.

4. Reading and writing are integrally related.

5. Learning increases when students collaborate in the learning process.

Miller (1999) asserts that many content area texts are written above grade level, and they are not written in a "reader friendly" fashion since they are usually written by experts in the content area. They often contain difficult concepts and may be uninteresting to students, especially those with little prior knowledge of the subject.

Vacca and Vacca (1999) feel that most middle and high school teachers still use the "assign and tell method." They assign a portion of a content-area-book chapter for the students to read, and then they tell them what they have read—mainly because the students are not interested and do not understand the assigned reading. It is especially difficult to reach all students in content area classes because of a wide range of abilities, motivation, and backgrounds.

Teachers in content area subjects must first discover what prior knowledge their students have regarding the topic. Next they must bring in a variety of materials—especially trade books—in order to make the content area subject matter more interesting and understandable. They must be prepared to teach their students reading strategies with regard to vocabulary studies and comprehension in order for the students to be successful in the class.

Professional Discussion Questions

1. Do content area teachers survey students to determine their prior knowledge of a topic before beginning?

2. Do content area teachers provide strategies for students with regard to vocabulary and comprehension?

3. Are students taught how to do effective research using the Internet?

4. Do content area teachers use trade books as resources?

5. Does the school media specialist provide lists of other available resources to content area subject teachers?

6. Do content areas teachers focus only on covering curriculum?

Practical Application

Content Area Reading Strategies

▣ Vocabulary Study

Use context to determine meaning.

Use words in sentences and paragraphs.

Use vocabulary words in writing summaries to demonstrate understanding.

Use semantic and concept maps to make connections with vocabulary words.

Use vocabulary words in a learning log.

Do not assign lists of vocabulary words to be "looked up" and memorized.

▣ Comprehension

Always assess prior knowledge (K-W-L, factual questions, mapping).

Use prediction and self-questioning techniques for understanding.

Summarize in written or oral format in order to check understanding.

Use the SQ3R method to check comprehension.

Make use of typographical cues (bold print, italics, headings, charts, graphs, etc.).

Model think-alouds.

Use graphic organizers to construct meaning.

Outline in order to review.

Use group discussions and discussion webs to clarify meaning.

Use pair reading.

Use resource books—such as picture books—to clarify.

Annotated Young Adult Literature

Abelove, Joan. *Go and Come Back.* DK Publishing Inc., 1998.

The author lived in the Amazon jungle for two years. This fictional story is about two young anthropologists who ask to live in the village of Poincushmana for one year. Alicia is a young female in the tribe who adopts an unwanted baby and tells of life in the tribe. The anthropologists, who come to study the ways of the people, learn from them as well. "In the end, at the end of it all, the love you have, the friendship you have, the love you are left with, is just the same, is only the same, as the love you gave, the love, the friendship you had for others."

Anderson, Laurie Halse. *Fever 1793.* Simon & Schuster Books for Young Readers, 2000.

Matilda is 16 years old and helps her mother and grandfather in the family-owned coffeehouse. When her mother becomes ill, Matilda is sent away to the countryside in order to escape the dreaded yellow fever. Ten miles outside of Philadelphia, Matilda and her grandfather are turned back and are not permitted to leave the city. After her grandfather dies as the result of a robbery, Matilda struggles to survive one of the worst epidemics in U.S. history.

Cooper, Susan. *King of Shadows.* Margaret K. McElderry Books, 1999.

Nat Field's short life has been shadowed by loss, but he is thrilled to be selected by an international director to perform at Shakespeare's Globe—London's amazing copy of the 400-year-old theater. While rehearsing in London, Nat becomes very ill and travels back in time to 1599 and performs at the Globe Theater along with Shakespeare. He develops a close relationship with Shakespeare and is devastated to leave him when he returns to the present. He discovers that the switch was necessary because the "other" Nat Field had bubonic plague, and if he hadn't left, Shakespeare would have contracted the disease and died.

Crew, Linda. *Children of the River.* Delacorte Press, 1989.

Sundara's parents sheltered her from the war and spirited her away from Phnom Penh to her aunt and uncle's fishing village. Two weeks later Sundara, 13, fled Cambodia with her aunt, uncle, grandmother, and cousins to escape the Khmer Rouge army.

Three weeks at sea and the responsibility of a small baby left Sundara struggling with guilt. She could not go home to her land and people. Now, four years later, she must adjust to her new life in Oregon. Jonathan, the star football player begins to interview Sundara for an international project. Sundara knows that she should follow Cambodian customs and not even talk to a boy. After many hardships and sorrows, Sundara finds peace with her aunt and uncle. She hopes that she will be reunited with her younger sister, and Jonathan, her love.

Jimenez, Francisco. *Circuits: Stories from the Life of a Migrant Child.* University of New Mexico Press, 1997.

Short stories tell the life of a migrant child and his family, filled with hope, sorrow, hardships, anger, and love. The author was second of seven brothers and sisters. At a very early age he was responsible for the care of his younger siblings while his parents and older brother would work in the fields picking either cotton, strawberries, or grapes in California. He went to school when he could be spared from the fields. The family moved to where work was available and lived in tents, garages, or barracks. When Francisco was in fifth grade he was invited over to a school friend's house. It was the first time he had been inside a house. The stories of this award-winning book give one a glimpse of the struggle and hardships of the American Dream.

Lasky, Kathryn. *Elizabeth I, Red Rose of the House of Tudor.* Scholastic Incorporated, 1999.

Elizabeth I was the forgotten princess of King Henry VIII and Anne Boleyn. Anne Boleyn was beheaded when Elizabeth was 3 and the belief that her mother was a witch haunted the girl. Told in diary form, Elizabeth struggles for attention from her father and fears her sister, Mary, and is concerned for the future king, sickly Edward VI. This novel ends with the death of Henry VIII but conveys a strong sense of intrigue and conspiracy on the part of Mary. Ultimately Elizabeth I will survive, become queen, and rule for nearly 15 years.

Lerangis, Peter. *Antarctica: Journey to the Pole.* Scholastic Incorporated, 2000.

This is part one of a two-part fictional series about a secret journey to discover the South Pole in 1909. This high adventure novel is filled with many exciting sea adventures, which include a stowaway, being trapped in an ice floe, getting lost in a blizzard, and a mutiny. The best part about reading this fictional account is that the reader has part two, *Escape from Disaster,* to look forward to.

Matcheck, Diane. *The Sacrifice.* Farrar Straus and Giroux, 1998.

A great example of survival fiction, this is the story of a 15-year-old Crow Indian girl who is left an orphan after the death of her father. She sets out on a quest to prove herself as a hunter and survivor, to avenge her father's death, and to prove that she, not her dead twin brother, is the Great One. The story takes place on the Great Plains in the 1700s. The girl wins a battle with a grizzly bear and makes a necklace of his claws and a cloak of his fur. She is taken prisoner by a band of Pawnees who treat her with respect. She falls in love with the boy who is her keeper, but she is horrified to learn that she is being prepared to be a sacrifice to the Morning Star.

Opdyke, Irene Gut. *In My Hands: Memories of a Holocaust Rescuer.* Alfred A. Knopf, 1999.

One of the Jews that Irene saved from the Holocaust said to Irene, "You're only a young girl. What can you do?" He was right, she was only a girl, alone among the enemy. Irene saved many lives by passing information to the nearby ghetto. She was personally responsible for saving 12 Jews by hiding them in the basement of the German major's villa until the Russians freed Poland. In March 1944 Irene was 22 and became a partisan who fought against Poland's enemies—both the Germans and the Russians. Ironically, it was her Jewish friends who took care of and saved Irene from the Communist Russians and sent her on to Germany to a repatriation camp for displaced persons. Irene has received international recognition for her actions and received Israel's highest tribute, Israel's Medal of Honor. In the dedication, Irene dedicates her life story to encourage young people "to find hope and strength within themselves. Courage is a whisper from above: when you listen with your heart, you will know what to do and how and when."

Paulsen, Gary. *Soldier's Heart.* Delacorte Press, 1998.

The subtitle reads, "being the story of the enlistment and due service of the boy Charley Goddard in the First Minnesota volunteers."

Men who have survived a war and carry permanent mental damage are known by different terms throughout history. After Vietnam, this condition was termed post-traumatic stress disorder. In the Civil War era, it was called soldier's heart.

Charley, 15, lies about his age and enlists in the Northern Army. He soon learns the realities of war after the flags and young girls stop waving. He survives four battles, from Bull Run to Gettysburg—but will he survive past 21 now that he is physically and emotionally damaged? Charley is too old, "old from too much life, old from seeing too much, old from knowing too much."

Smith, Roland. *Jaguar.* Hyperion Books for Children, 1997.

Jaguar is an exciting adventure and ecological novel. Jake is a freshman in high school who is left behind when his father, Doc, travels to the Amazon jungle to set up a jaguar preserve. After months of no contact, Jake receives a fax and a promise of an airline ticket, which leads to months in the Amazon tracking jaguars in an ultralight and avoiding Tyler, who is searching for the lost gold mines of Muribeca. *Jaguar* is action-filled and winner of the 2000 Sunshine State Young Readers Award.

Springer, Nancy. *I Am Mordred: A Tale from Camelot.* Philomel Books, 1998.

Mordred is the nephew and son of King Arthur. According to Merlin, it is Mordred's fate to kill Arthur in the midst of a battle. Arthur tries to avoid this fate by taking all the male babies, putting them in a boat, and sending them out to sea to die. A fisherman finds Mordred and raises him until Nyneve, a sorceress, takes him away and leaves him with his mother. Mordred grows to be a man and a knight of the Round Table. Mordred thinks that if Arthur recognizes him as his son, fate will be thwarted and love will be his salvation.

Wilson, Diane Lee. *I Rode a Horse of Milk White Jade.* Orchard Books, 1998.

Born on the Mongolian steppes during the reign of Kublai Khan (1339), as an infant Oyuna's foot is crushed by a horse, and her clan believes she is cursed with bad luck. At 13 she sets off on a journey disguised as a boy with her white mare and her cat. Oyuna has a special gift with horses; sometimes she can hear her mare speak. She goes in search of the perfect white horse belonging to Kublai Khan so that she can win a race. The story is told by an elderly Oyuna to her granddaughter as they await the birth of a foal—a direct descendant of Oyuna's beloved mare in the story.

Annotated Professional Journal Articles

Barr, Katherine. "Content Area Reading: An Apprenticeship Model," *The Florida Reading Quarterly* (June 2000): 6-8.

The author claims that students can master effective reading strategies when the teachers model their use and engage students in discussions that build metacognitive awareness. The eight strategies covered in the article are relate, react, picture, summarize, question, predict, clarify, and describe the significance.

Burton, Mary Lee. "Addressing the Literacy Crisis: Teaching Reading in the Content Areas," *National Association of Secondary School Principals Publication* (March 1997): 42-50.

Reading skills are taught only in the elementary school. When a student reaches middle school he or she is forced to make the change from learning to read to reading to learn without much help. This article describes a strategic reader as one who

- ▸▸ actively works to construct meaning,

- ▸▸ employs specific tactics for reading texts,

- ▸▸ relies on prior knowledge,

- ▸▸ uses text features—headings, bold type, vocabulary, and text structure—to increase comprehension, and

- ▸▸ possesses a variety of text-processing strategies that help plan, monitor, control, and evaluate reading.

The author states that every content area teacher should be teaching all students these strategies.

Holloway, John. "Improving the Reading Skills of Adolescents," *Educational Leadership* (October 1999): 80-81.

According to this article, in order to improve the reading skills of adolescents it is necessary to connect content reading assignments to real-world learning experiences. Teachers should give students self-directed activities, invite collaborative learning, and allow for varied forms of self-expression. Teachers are encouraged to read to their adolescent students and to make reading enjoyable. "The only way to improve reading skills is to read."

Irvin, Judith. "Invisible Demands on Young Adolescents: Dealing with Expository Text,"
SIGNAL (January 1997): 6-7.

Textbooks are more abundant and more difficult in the middle grades. Students are expected to understand texts with less assistance from the teacher—little time is spent teaching students the hierarchical patterns of main idea and details. In the middle grades, not only language arts teachers, but also science and social studies teachers, need to provide students with effective strategies for reading expository texts.

Klemp, Ronald. "Using the Directed Reading Sequence as an Interactive Strategy in Content
Area Reading," *Middle School Journal* (May 1997): 46-49.

Klemp shares a specific strategy for successful content area reading. Directed reading sequence is a small-group cooperative learning activity. Each student in the group has a role: paraphraser, verifier, squeezer (summarizer), and writer. The roles are rotated, and the students are instructed to help each other with understanding the text. This strategy has proven to be successful.

Simmons, John S. "Ways to Boost Student Literacy in the Information Age," *The Florida
Reading Quarterly* (June 2000): 26-29, 36.

Nine ways to help students with reading content area texts and survival documents are shared by the author. They include finding meanings of abstract terms, technical terms, metaphors, translation of symbols, relating word groups as modifiers, cross-referencing, finding cause/effect relationships, explicit meaning, and implied meaning. The sample applications are excellent.

Annotated Professional Books

Beers, Kylene, and Barbara Samuels, eds. *Into Focus: Understanding and Creating Middle
School Readers.* Christopher-Gordon, 1998.

There are 22 essays in this volume written by 27 authors on a wide variety of topics of interest to those working with middle school students. The topics include understanding middle school students, choosing not to read, gifted middle school readers, struggling readers, reader response theory, thematic units and readers workshop, literature discussions, literature circles, journals, content area reading, authentic reading assessment, short stories, novels, and reading and the Internet.

Billmeyer, Rachel, and Mary Lee Barton. *Teaching Reading in the Content Areas: If Not Me,
Then Who?* McREL, 1998.

A graphic organizer showing the three interactive elements of reading and the six assumptions about learning introduces this book. It goes on to discuss each element and assumption. The book ends with a complete and useful bibliography. This is an excellent resource filled with strategies for all content area teachers who know the importance of reading and want to help their students to read more effectively.

Borasi, Raffaella, and Marjorie Siegel. *Reading Counts: Expanding the Role of Reading in
Mathematics Classrooms.* Teachers College Press, 2000.

Reading Counts begins with frameworks for rethinking reading in mathematics instruction—including one for inquiry-oriented instruction and rethinking reading theory and practice. There is an overview of the Reading to Learn Mathematics Project, with follow-up studies. Several sample inquiry cycles are highlighted.

Harvey, Stephanie. *Nonfiction Matters: Reading, Writing, and Research in Grades 3-8.* Stenhouse Publishers, 1998.

Several conditions must be present for successful inquiry: compelling questions, good topics, authentic resources, and effective directions. This book includes sections on how to read nonfiction, do research, observe and organize, and assess nonfiction and inquiry projects. There are extensive appendixes with forms, lists, and complete bibliographies by topic.

Harvey, Stephanie, and Anne Goudvis. *Strategies That Work: Teaching Comprehension to Enhance Understanding.* Stenhouse Publishers, 2000.

All aspects of comprehension, beginning with the foundation of meaning, are highlighted. Many different strategy lessons, including making connections, questioning, visualizing, inferring, determining importance in nonfiction, synthesizing information, instruction in context, and assessing comprehension, are featured. The book has an excellent resource section with lists of great books and authors; specific lists of books for teaching content in history, social studies, science, music, art, and literacy; texts for adults; lists of magazines and newspapers; professional journals for the selection of children's books; and a response option for each strategy.

McElmeel, Sharron. *Great New Nonfiction Reads.* Libraries Unlimited, 1995.

To determine an information book's potential appeal one needs to consider the attractiveness of the cover, the credibility of the author, the copyright date, whether the book gives accurate information on all sides of the topic, the accuracy of the graphics, and the book's organization. This book encourages the reading of nonfiction books aloud and responding. It even includes 25 general ideas for responses. The majority of the book lists nonfiction titles, some annotated, by topics.

Miller, Wilma. *Ready-to-Use Activities and Materials for Improving Content Reading Skills.* Prentice-Hall, 1999.

This practical resource for grades 4 through 12 classroom teachers is packed with hundreds of strategies and reproducible activity sheets for evaluating, and improving students' reading, writing, study, and test-taking skills in the content areas (language arts, social studies, science, and mathematics).

Vacca, Richard, and JoAnne Vacca. *Content Area Reading: Literacy and Learning Across the Curriculum.* Addison-Wesley Longman, 1999.

This college text is an excellent and often-quoted resource for content area reading. The chapters include teaching and learning with texts, strategy instruction in diverse classrooms, integrating electronic texts and trade books into the curriculum, making authentic assessments, bringing students and texts together, talking and writing to learn, vocabulary and concepts, prior knowledge and interest, study strategies and guides, and growth and reflection in the teaching profession.

Web Sites

The Arts

ArtsEdge at Kennedy Center
   http://artsedge.kennedy-center.org/

Bayly African Art Museum
   http://www.lib.virginia.edu/dic/exhib/93.ray.aa/African.html

Fine Art Forum
   http://www.msstate.edu/Fineart_Online/art-resources/museums.html

Paleolithic Cave Paintings in France
   http://www.culture.fr/culture/arcnat/chauvet/en/gvpda-d.htm

Smithsonian American Art Museum
   http://www.nmaa.si.edu/

Theatre History on the Web
   http://www.artsci.washington.edu/drama/jack.html

World Wide Art Resources
   http://wwar.com/

English Language Arts

Definition Guessing Game—Fake Out!
   http://www.eduplace.com/dictionary/

English Exercises Online
   http://www.smic.be/smic5022/

The Five Paragraph Essay Wizard
   http://www.geocities.com/SoHo/Atrium/1437/index.html

The Grammar Lady
   http://www.grammarlady.com/

Inkspot's Resources for Young Writers
   http://www.inkspot.com/young/

Kid Bibs
   http://kidbibs.com/home.htm

Kids' Space
   http://www.kids-space.org/

Schoolhouse Rock
   http://genxtvland.simplenet.com/SchoolHouseRock/

Vocabulary Study
   http://www.srv.net/~allenh/leave/vocab_study.html

Vocabulary University
   http://www.vocabulary.com/

Word Play
    http://www.wolinskyweb.com/word.htm

The Write Site
    http://www.writesite.org/

Literature

BookHive: Guide to Children's Literature
    http://www.bookhive.org/bookhive.htm

Database of Award Winning Children's Literature
    http://www2.wcoil.com/~ellerbee/childlit.html

Personal Web Site of Author Brian Jacques
    http://www.redwall.org/dave/jacques.html

Picture Books for Older Readers
    http://www.beyondbasals.com/older.html

The Reading Village
    http://teams.lacoe.edu/village/

Sacramento Public Library Teens Pages
    http://www.saclibrary.org/teens/default.asp

SCORE CyberGuides
    http://www.sdcoe.k12.ca.us/score/cyberguide.html

Vandergrift's Young Adult Literature Page
    http://www.scils.rutgers.edu/special/kay/yalit.html

Mathematics

Color Math Pink—Math for Girls
    http://www.colormathpink.com/

Dave's Math Tables
    http://www.sisweb.com/math/tables.htm

FunBrain Math Games
    http://www.funbrain.com/numbers.html

The Geometry Center
    http://www.geom.umn.edu/

Math Archives
    http://archives.math.utk.edu/

The Math Forum
    http://forum.swarthmore.edu/

Math in Daily Life
    http://www.learner.org/exhibits/dailymath/

Math Is Fun
http://www.mathsisfun.com/

Math Nerds
http://www.mathnerds.com/

Math Stories
http://www.mathstories.com/

The Math Zone
http://www.zone101.com/LearningZone/MathZones/mathzones.htm

Mega-Mathematics
http://www.cs.uidaho.edu/~casey931/mega-math/

Science

Ask Dr. Universe
http://www.wsu.edu/DrUniverse

Bill Nye
http://nyelabs.kcts.org/f_index.html

Bugscope
http://bugscope.beckman.uiuc.edu/

eNature
http://www.enature.com/

Skeletons
http://www.eskeletons.org/

How Stuff Works
http://www.howstuffworks.com/

The Mad Scientist's Network
http://www.madsci.org/

NASA's Observatorium
http://observe.ivv.nasa.gov/nasa/core.shtml.html

SeaWorld/Busch Gardens Animal Information
http://www.seaworld.org/

Skateboard Science
http://www.exploratorium.edu/skateboarding/

Virtual Field Trips
http://www.field-guides.com/

Volcanoes Online
http://library.advanced.org/tq-admin/month.cgi

Weather Eye
http://weathereye.kgan.com/

The Why Files
http://whyfiles.org/

Xpeditions
http://www.nationalgeographic.com/xpeditions/main.html

The Yuckiest Site on the Internet
http://www.yucky.com/

Social Studies

America's Library
http://www.americaslibrary.gov/cgi-bin/page.cgi

The Ancient World
http://www.julen.net/ancient/

Ben's Guide to the US Government
http://bensguide.gpo.gov/

Biographies of America's Founding Fathers
http://www.colonialhall.com/index.asp

The Field Museum of Chicago
http://www.fmnh.org/

Flag Tag Game
http://www.un.org/Pubs/CyberSchoolBus/flagtag/index.html

Great American Speeches
http://www.pbs.org/greatspeeches/

History Central
http://www.historycentral.com/index.html

The History Net
http://www.thehistorynet.com/

History/Social Studies Web Site for K-12 Teachers
http://www.execpc.com/~dboals/boals.html

Mapping the World by Heart
http://www.mapping.com/

National Council on Economic Education
http://www.nationalcouncil.org/

United States Thematic Maps
http://www.oseda.missouri.edu/graphics/us/

World Surfari
http://www.supersurf.com/

12

Information Literacy

Information literacy includes the planning, processing, and the thinking skills needed in order to make use of information available from multiple formats, including books, newspapers, magazines, videos, reference works, electronic indexes, CD-ROMs, and the Internet. In prior years, librarians taught library skills. Now media specialists teach informational skills integrated with the curriculum. These skills are not taught in isolation, but on an as-needed basis.

"Successful integrated information skills programs are designed around collaborative projects planned and taught by teachers and library media specialists," state Eisenberg and Johnson (1996). Valenza (1996) says, "Computer literacy is not information literary." "Library media specialists, computer teachers, and classroom teachers need to work together to develop units and lessons that will include computer skills, general information skills, and content-area curriculum outcomes," say Eisenberg and Johnson (1996). The American Library Association has developed nine information literacy standards to empower student learning (http://www.ala.org/aasl/ip_nine.html). These standards emphasize information literacy, independent learning, and social responsibility. Students must be able to select, access, evaluate, and synthesize information using various sources and mediums.

Eisenberg and Johnson (1996) state that in 1992, Christina Doyle described an information-literate person in her Final Report to the National Forum on Information Literacy as one who

- recognizes that accurate and complete information is the basis for intelligent decision making,

- recognizes the need for information,

- formulates questions based on information needs,

- identifies potential sources of information,

- develops successful search strategies,

- accesses sources of information, including computer-based and other technologies,

- evaluates information,

- organizes information for practical application,

►► integrates new information into an existing body of knowledge, and

►► uses information in critical thinking and problem solving.

These standards are goals to strive for, and we need to empower students with a process to solve problems and access information. Information skills need to be tied to the school's curriculum and incorporate information process models such as the Big Six®, Pathways to Knowledge, or FLIP IT. The Big Six® was developed by Michael B. Eisenberg and Robert E. Berkowitz to identify what information one wants to know, locate, understand, evaluate, and use in an efficient and logical manner. This model will follow students throughout their educational and work career. The Big Six® information problem-solving approach is as follows:

►► Task Definition

►► Information Seeking Strategies

►► Location and Access

►► Use of Information

►► Synthesis

►► Evaluation

Marjorie Pappas and Ann Tepe emphasized research stages in their Pathways to Knowledge model. These stages are presearch, search, interpretation, communication, and evaluation. Pappas (1997) uses graphic organizers to "provide learners with a visual structure that allows them to make connections between topics or concepts, relate to prior knowledge, plan a search strategy, select and evaluate information, interpret information, and evaluate the research outcomes." This is a nonlinear model, and each stage contains both general and specific strategies to aid the researcher. One can begin at any stage, and evaluation is an ongoing process that cuts across all the stages.

Alice H. Yucht developed FLIP IT, a four-step problem process to help solve present as well as future problems. FLIP IT is a mnemonic to keep the researcher on task. This is a four-step process that asks the following questions:

►► Focus—What is the quest that I am on?

►► Links—What prior knowledge can I use?

►► Input—What kind of information do I need to gather?

►► Payoff—How do I put it all together?

This model uses the same strategies as other models, but it puts it together in a language that kids understand. Yucht (1999) says, "At each step the learner needs to re-focus on the original concerns to make sure that the target questions are being answered and acted upon." At each step the researcher uses all four steps to keep the research on track. Each step leads to the next step; it is a circular process.

No matter which research process your school decides on, the skills should be modeled numerous times before this process is used to solve all kinds of problems, both now and in the future. Students acquire information literacy skills as a result of collaborative teaching by classroom teachers and the library media specialists. These abstract models should be teacher/librarian guided as part of a research/information need or an assigned project. Doug Johnson (1999) states that there are four As that one must consider when designing research projects that teachers and students will find enjoyable. These four As are as follows:

◄◄ Assignments that matter

◄◄ Activities that involve the researcher

◄◄ Assessments that help by promoting growth and showing care

◄◄ (Teacher) Attitude is everything

Teachers can help students avoid plagiarism by designing projects that give students choices, use higher level thinking skills, and solve real problems or apply ideas. The process should be emphasized with built-in checks along the way, such as outlines, drafts, and working bibliographies and copies of applicable research. Ask students to reflect on the research process and assignment. Teachers and librarians must take an active role in the research process and give students clear expectations, goals, time frames, and methods to produce an end product they are proud of. This product may be in the form of a paper, multi-media presentation, experiment, art form, skit, or video. A rubric should be provided that describes differing levels of competency so students have a clear idea of the expectations and attainable goals. Having successful library projects takes preplanning and cooperation with the teacher, adequate resources, attainable and authentic requirements, and the research skills and process to do the project.

Professional Discussion Questions

1. Do you have a research process model that is used across the curriculum?

2. Is detecting a plagiarist an impossible task for teachers? What means should teachers take to prevent and check on plagiarism?

3. What is authentic assessment? What are the information literacy outcome goals you want your students to accomplish? Are they defined by grade level?

4. Who evaluates your library media center? Does it have adequate resources? Is it flexibly scheduled?

Annotated Professional Journal Articles

Anderson, Mary Alice. "Changing Roles, Changing Programs," *The Book Report* (September/October 1995): 17.

The changing role of the media specialist means a change in programs. There will be an increased number of students using the media center. Circulation of books, magazines, and so forth, may be down because students gain their information from electronic resources. As the demand for services grows, access to the media center becomes a challenge and may result in longer hours of operation. Technology is changing how librarians spend their time. The results are exciting and challenging.

Anderson, Mary Alice. "The Impact of the Internet," *The Book Report* (May/June 1997): 27-28.

The Internet has led to many positive experiences:

▸▸ Students will readily use the Internet search engines when they won't or cannot use an index to a book.

▸▸ Teachers teach and students learn differently.

▸▸ Cooperative group work is more common.

▸▸ Learning is of greater quality, even though sometimes less is covered.

▸▸ Library circulation is up.

▸▸ Students learn skills that can be applied to other technologies.

▸▸ Community and parental support is enhanced.

As we become more proficient in Internet usage, we will take advantage of its full capabilities, and students will learn that it is simply another tool and not the answer to every information need.

Barron, Daniel D. "Families, Technology, and Literacy: Roles and Research Resources for School Library Media Specialists (Part 1)," *School Library Media Activities Monthly* (December 1996): 47-50.

Everyone must have equal access to technology and information systems. Until that happens, we have "Educational Apartheid." This access to information is critical in our schools, communities, and families. We must help our families become literate in both technology and print. The article includes short summaries of reports that will be useful to meet the challenges of family involvement and educating our youth.

Baule, Steve. "Easy to Find but Not Necessarily True," *The Book Report* (September/October 1997): 26.

As librarians and teachers, we should teach students to use the best source, be it print or Internet based. Students using the web must use four criteria to evaluate the information they find:

1. Purpose of the article or information
2. Author's credibility
3. Publication date and date of updates
4. Wording of site titles

Boardman, Edna M. "How to Help Students Deal with 'Too Much Information,' " *The Book Report* (September/October 1995): 23-24.

"The challenge is not to find something 'about' their chosen topic but to determine what will fill their needs." Teachers and librarians need to:

◄◄ keep students from reverting to the same tired topics when presented with too much information,

◄◄ pay attention to how students are selecting their topics,

◄◄ help students in the process of selecting material from all the information available,

◄◄ help students evaluate sources,

◄◄ help students narrow the topic, but not so much that nothing can be found, and

◄◄ help students explore the indexes,

We must take a proactive role in helping students deal will the quantity and quality of material available.

Boardman, Edna M. "Another Viewpoint: We Need Two Libraries: One Electronic, One Book," *The Book Report* (March/April 1996): 17.

"We need to let computers do what they do best and let print do what it does best." We must support and enrich both types of media in the library. We must be clear in the goals for both electronic information and print information. Both serve a purpose, and we should take care that computers do not dominate because of our neglect or leaving things to chance.

Callison, Daniel. "Key Term: Questioning," *School Library Media Activities Monthly* (February 1997): 30-31.

The library media center is the best place for students to raise questions, reveal their thoughts, and help organize their thinking. Finding answers to questions through reading, viewing, and discussion should lead to further questioning.
The library media specialist should

◄◄ model questioning,

◄◄ engage students in sharing their questions and resources,

◄◄ look for a variety of questions that encourage higher level thinking skills,

◄◄ recognize a good question and state why it is good,

◀ display questions for students,

◀ organize the Dewey Decimal system with the aid of questions,

◀ end booktalks with questions,

◀ encourage teachers to organize their units by essential questions that will lead to further exploration,

◀ do not ask all the questions, and

◀ leave enough time for students to answer the questions.

Collins, Joan. "Media Literacy: From Viewing to Doing," *The Book Report* (September/October 1999): 23-24.

Students, teachers, and media specialists planned, researched, organized, and evaluated information to create a web page for incoming sixth graders. They created an exciting, animated web site to communicate to fifth graders what it was like to be in middle school.

Eisenberg, Michael B., and Doug Johnson. "Computer Skills for Information Problem-Solving: Learning and Teaching Technology in Context," *ERIC Digest* (March 1996).

Computer skills should not be taught in isolation—this is something that media specialists can relate to. Computer skills should be integrated into the curriculum and classroom assignments. "Information literacy is the ability to access, evaluate, and use information from multiple formats." The article includes a suggested computer skill curriculum, based on the Big Six® approaches.

Everhart, Nancy. "Evaluating School Library Information Services in the Digital Age," *The Book Report* (January/February 2000): 58-60.

School library media services are effectively evaluated because of the technology available. In many states, departments of education provide a checklist of expected services, and the American Association of School Librarians is planning a national rubric. Surveys, interviews, and focus-group interviews determine how the services are being received. Facilities, usage, circulation, changes due to technology, fill rate, OPAC station reports, observations, and student work are other areas to examine.

Farmer, Lesley S. J. "Authentic Assessment of Information Literacy through Electronic Products," *The Book Report* (September/October 1997): 11-13.

Outcome based education that uses authentic assessment is one way to document what students learn. Outcomes describe the performance and content standard students will meet. "Outcomes need to be authentic: that is, true to life and reflect lifelong learning skills. Outcomes should also answer essential questions and use higher-order thinking skills." The assessment to measure the outcomes may take the form of a product, performance, or process. Assessment is an ongoing activity. A rubric is used to evaluate the different levels of competencies. Information literacy skills are essential to outcome based learning. Included are several examples of how to introduce authentic assessment.

Harada, Violet H. "Presearch Before Research: A Vital Connection," *School Library Media Activities Monthly* (June 1997): 31-33.

The Big Six® identifies this portion of the research process as identifying the information need. Teachers and librarians must help motivate students in their investigation and provide library time for browsing and exploration. Thoughtful discussion and decision making should be encouraged. The author provides a model to follow.

Jansen, Barbara A. "Using the Big Six® Research Process: The Coconut Crab from Guam and Other Stories," *MultiMedia Schools* (November/December 1996): 32-37.

A practical step-by-step application of the Big Six® research process used in a combined gifted class of third, fourth, and fifth grades. Using this model they communicated with other students from around the world and wrote original folktales using the acquired information.

Johnson, Doug. "Designing Research Projects Students (and Teachers) Love," *MultiMedia Schools* (November/December 1999): 37-42.

Designing research projects requires careful planning, and the projects share three characteristics:

1. Assignments that matter
   ◄◄ Clarity of purpose and expectations
   ◄◄ Student choice
   ◄◄ Relevant to their life
   ◄◄ Higher level thinking skills and creativity
   ◄◄ Answer real questions

2. Activities that involve the researcher
   ◄◄ Variety of information-finding activities
   ◄◄ Hands-on
   ◄◄ Exciting programs
   ◄◄ Formats that use multiple senses of sight and sound
   ◄◄ Complex projects broken down into smaller steps
   ◄◄ Group work results are usually better than individual

3. Assessments that help by promoting growth and showing concern
   ◄◄ Results shared with people who care and respond
   ◄◄ Rubrics and checklists used
   ◄◄ Samples and examples show what quality work looks like
   ◄◄ Learner reflects, revisits, revises, and improves final projects

The key to good research projects is the attitude of the teacher.

- ◀◀ Okay with loss of control over time, final product, and "correct" answers

- ◀◀ Active rather than passive students

- ◀◀ All students capable of high performance, given enough time, resources, and motivation

- ◀◀ Expertise in the learning and research process rather than a particular subject area

- ◀◀ Teacher enthusiasm very important

- ◀◀ Not all projects will work first time—learn what went well and carefully prepare the next project

Lewin, Larry. " 'Site Reading' the World Wide Web." *Educational Leadership* (February 1999): 16-20.

Students benefit by using the Web and the Internet. We must help our students "site read." Students read for understanding by using an electronic e-sheet complete with guided questions to answer on their floppy disks. To read for deeper meaning the author reformats and breaks down the selected web site. He uses questions and embedded hints and copies it all to a disk. The author of the web site is critiqued by students who look at multiple sources and compare and contrast their reactions. Using these techniques will help student become careful and skillful readers of the Web.

Milbury, Peter. "Effective Searching Buys Time to Reflect, Ponder & Analyze," *The Book Report* (September/October 1997): 23-24.

Students use models such as the Big Six® to help organize and process information. Librarians have a responsibility to "make information available in an effective and well-organized manner." One way to do this is to create a web page organized by curriculum with links to subjects that are constantly revised and reorganized. A key to this process is the librarian's outreach to teachers by sharing new web sites; sharing technology expertise; and planning interviews before all classes are brought to the library.

Murray, Janet. "From School Librarian to 'Information TeAchnician': A Challenge for the Information Age," *Library Talk* (May/June 1999): 10-13.

Too much emphasis has been put on technological hardware, infrastructure, and data. "Experienced educators know that we must add an 'A' to 'tech'; technology in isolation ignores the 'A' in 'teAch.' " Librarians are in a pivotal position to implement the ALA's Information Power's nine standards and 29 indicators of proficiency in information literacy. The article includes a discussion of 24 useful web sites, tutorials, and books to help the librarian become an information specialist.

Pappas, Marjorie L. "Making Sense of Interpretation through Graphic Organizers," *School Library Media Activities Monthly* (June 1996): 36-38.

Students are able to gather a vast amount of information, but information alone is not knowledge. Teachers and librarians should develop strategies to help students interpret and reflect on the acquired information. General graphic organizers assist students in their active learning and organizing of new knowledge. Three sample graphic organizers are included.

Pappas, Marjorie L. "Organizing Research," *School Library Media Activities Monthly* (December 1997): 30-32.

The author explains the Information Skills Organizer Chart and the importance of using this structure with children to "enable them to explore relationships, organize information, and think critically."

Rankin, Virginia. "The Thought that Counts: Six Skills that Help Kids Turn Notes into Knowledge," *School Library Journal* (August 1999): 27-29.

Rankin uses graphic organizers and extension questions to assist students when they are using higher level thinking skills. Examples are given for each of the six skills:

1. Compare and contrast: uses T-Chart or Venn diagram organizers

2. Sequencing: uses flow chart organizers

3. Classifying: uses web organizers

4. Cause and effect: uses cause and effect circles

5. Problem solving: uses chart organizers

6. Decision making: uses chart organizers

Renard, Lisa. "Cut and Paste 101: Plagiarism and the Net," *Educational Leadership* (December 1999/January 2000): 38-43.

"Cut and Paste" has made it easy for students to plagiarize and use technology dishonestly. The author describes three types of cheaters:

1. The Unintentional Cheater: students who do not document their resources after copying word for word.

2. The Sneaky Cheater: students who knowingly plagiarize and work hard to cover it up.

3. The All-or-Nothing cheater: student takes a paper off the Net word for word as if it were his or her own work. This is the easiest to detect.

Teachers must be involved in the writing process and provide good assignments that use higher level thinking skills, model documentation, and personalize the assignment. Prevention is more important than catching cheaters.

Turrell, Linda G. "Designing the New Library Computer Skills Curriculum," *School Library Media Activities Monthly* (November 1997): 36-38.

What are the goals and skills that we want our students to have at each grade level? These goals need to be defined and supported. What are the desired student outcomes, or what do we want students to be able to do with this new technology? Students should

- ◂◂ design an effective research question,

- ◂◂ understand a database,

- ◂◂ design simple search strategies,

- ◂◂ design more advanced search strategies,

- ◂◂ understand a computer citation/abstract, and

- ◂◂ document computer resources.

Valenza, Joyce Kasman. "Information Literacy Is More Than Computer Literacy," *Philadelphia Online—Philadelphia Inquirer—More School News* (1996): http://crossings.phillynews .com/archive/k12/inforlit4_16.htm.

"Computer literacy is not information literacy." Students must be taught a process to handle and search for the information needed. They must be taught to synthesize the information and make use of it in meaningful ways. The new literacy standards developed by ALA will define the necessary skills in concrete terms.

Valenza, Joyce Kasman. "A Delicate Balance: The School Librarian and the Wired YA," *VOYA* (April 2000): 28.

Many students are not used to having an adult around who is familiar with computers and the Internet. As media specialists we must ensure that students become effective users of information. Oftentimes students do not think they need our help. We must be subtle and work one-on-one when searching problems arise.

Walker, Decker. "Technology and Literacy: Raising the Bar," *Educational Leadership* (October 1999): 18-21.

Information literacy is raising the bar in education. Some tasks will be simplified, and students will explore and use technology in new and different ways. When everyone achieves a particular skill level, then you push on to the next. Educated people will be "competent researchers and knowledge managers, keeping track of what they know and don't know and finding ways to learn what they need."

Wice, Nathaniel. "Copy and Paste: Term Paper Mills on the Web," *Y-Life* (January 1997).

"Eighty percent of undergraduates admitted to cheating at least once in surveys last year of more than two dozen colleges." Many Internet sites provide free access to term papers as well as commercial sites, which provide rush five-minute e-mail delivery. The sites are discussed. Teachers must look carefully at their assignments and pay attention to their students to avoid plagiarism.

Yucht, Alice H. "FLIP IT! For Information Skills Strategies," *The Book Report* (January/February 1999): 17-18.

The author developed a four-step information-skills problem-solving strategy in 1988. At the time, she was working with a group of seventh graders, and together they came up with a process called FLIP IT. "Student-centered FLIP IT! is based on the question 'What do I already know that will help me here?' "

◂◂ FOCUS (guideposts for the quest)
Questions help narrow the search and focus on the issues.

◂◂ LINKS (connections to help me proceed)
What resources should I use for locating the best information efficiently?

◂◂ INPUT (putting to use the information I've gathered)
What kinds of information do I need, how do I synthesize it and cite it?

◂◂ PAYOFF (putting it all together—for a profitable solution)
Have I solved my original problem, and how could I best communicate my results?

Annotated Professional Books

Benjamin, A. *An English Teacher's Guide to Performance Tasks and Rubrics: Middle School.* Eye on Education, 2000.

This book provides information on using performance tasks, including design elements, assessment, portfolios, and time management issues. It also describes rubrics, how to create and use them, common pitfalls, and design problems—too many, too general, too wordy, too much jargon. It tells how to use rubrics with standards, portfolios, and multiple intelligences. It includes a collection of performance tasks and rubrics for vocabulary, poetry, drama, speech, film, spelling, punctuation, language and cultural identity, novels, and the writing process.

Bromley, Karen, Linda DeVitis, and Marcia Modio. *50 Graphic Organizers for Reading, Writing & More.* Scholastic Professional Books, 1999.

Reproducible templates, student samples, and easy strategies to support every learner are examined. The introduction includes information on the definition of a graphic organizer, the different kinds, reasons for using them, what kind to use, making your own, grouping students, twelve FAQs regarding graphic organizers, and a long list of references.

Flynn, Kris. *Graphic Organizers . . . Helping Children Think Visually.* Creative Teaching Press, 1995.

Although this book was written for grades 3 through 6, the organizers could be adapted and used in middle school. The organizers are grouped by sequencing, brainstorming, classifying, identifying, creating, recording, mapping, comparing, and evaluating.

Forte, Imogene, and Sandra Schurr, *Graphic Organizers & Planning Outlines for Instruction and Assessment.* Incentive Publications, 1996.

This book contains many reproducible forms: grids, charts, graphs, cognitive taxonomy outlines, forms for group learning, forms for interdisciplinary teaching, planning forms and outlines, research and study aids, webs and writing planners, and organizers. There are detailed descriptions and suggestions for use.

Harvey, Stephanie. *Nonfiction Matters: Reading, Writing, and Research in Grades 3-8.* Stenhouse Publishers, 1998.

There are conditions for successful inquiry: compelling questions, good topics, authentic resources, and effective directions. This book includes sections on how to read nonfiction, do research, observe and organize, and assess nonfiction and inquiry projects. There are extensive appendixes with forms and lists and complete bibliographies by topic.

International Society for Technology in Education. *National Educational Technology Standards for Students.* ISTE, 2000.

Discussions about connecting curriculum and technology, essential conditions, the definition of curriculum integration, and information on how to use the book are included. The second section lists the technology standards for grades PK through 2, 3 through 5, 6 through 8, and 9 through 12 and includes profiles, performance indicators, curriculum examples, and scenarios. The third section contains specific examples of curriculum integration for all grade levels in these areas: language arts, foreign language, math, science, and social studies. The fourth section includes multidisciplinary resource units for all grade levels. There are complete appendixes with many resources for teachers and technology coordinators.

Jody, Marilyn, and Marianne Saccardi. *Using Computers to Teach Literature: A Teacher's Guide.* National Council of Teachers of English, 1998.

This guide discusses the BookRead Project, which connects classes and authors for online discussions of literature. It includes an annotated list of language arts web sites, author web sites, publishers' sites, staff development online, and books online. There are excerpts from online author chats and chats about certain readings. It includes an annotated bibliography of children's books and resources for teachers.

McElmeel, S., and C. Smallwood. *WWW Almanac: Making Curriculum Connections to Special Days, Weeks, and Months.* Linworth, 1999.

Literacy on the Web is featured and general occasions, celebrations, and literary events are highlighted. There is a month-by-month listing of special days and weeks, with appropriate web sites, including the author/sponsor of the site, information found on the site, and a summary of the contents, lessons, and ideas for curriculum connections.

Rief, Linda. *Vision and Voice: Extending the Literacy Spectrum.* Heinemann, 1999.

A CD showing finished projects with sound tracks is an added feature. Chapters include information about research—background information, formulating questions, and searching for answers. All projects have a rain forest/environmental theme and cover making bookmarks, pamphlets, and picture books.

Web Sites

Big Six® Skills to Information Problem Solving
http://ericir.syr.edu/big6/bigsix.html

Computer Skills for Information Problem Solving Based on the Big6 Skill Approach
http://ericir.syr.edu/ithome/digests/computerskills.html

Core Student Technology Skills
http://www.roanoke.k12.va.us/TP95/sect10.html

CTAP or California Technology Assistance Project Guidelines for K-12
http://ctap.fcoe.k12.ca.us/ctap/Info.Lit/infolit.html

Curriculum and Lesson Plans for Information Technology
http://www.wlma.org/literacy/curplan.htm

Digital High School Lists Links to Information Literacy and Technology Frameworks
http://www.schoolibrary.org/dhs/infolit.html

Directory of Online Resources for Information Literacy
http://www.cas.usf.edu/lis/il/process.html

Eisenberg's Big Six®
http://www.big6.com/

ICONnect—Service Helps Students Access and Use the Information Available on the
Internet Effectively and Efficiently. Also Offers Online Classes.
http://www.ala.org/ICONN/fc-infolit.html

Information Literacy Skills—Mankato (Minnesota) Schools
http://www.isd77.k12.mn.us/resources/infocurr/infolit.html

Lists of Links about Information Literacy
http://www.nexus.edu.au/TeachStud/lis/infolit.htm#Websites

National Forum on Informational Literacy
http://www.infolit.org/

Nine Information Literacy Standards for Student Learning
http://www.ala.org/aasl/ip_nine.html

Oregon Information Literacy Guidelines
http://www.teleport.com/~oema/infolit.html

Washington State Essential Skills for Information Literacy
http://www.wlma.org/literacy/eslintro.htm

13

The Reading Plan

Fully developing this plan in your school is an ongoing process. It is necessary to first identify the stakeholders in your school community. They should include all middle school teachers, the reading coach, the media specialist, the technology coordinator, and the administration. It is important to have the full support of the administration. It is necessary that everyone agrees on the significance of focusing on reading in the middle level grades. The chapters in this book can serve as workshops with the questions, articles, and information used to bring about discussion and change pertinent to your school community. The workshop format provides the opportunity to talk about new ideas and strategies that work and then apply them to your situation.

By developing and implementing your own school reading plan similar to this one, you are making the statement that you want your students to become lifelong readers. Students will realize the significance as well because of the time, effort, and commitment of those who put this plan into action.

In order to increase the chances that middle level students will read, it is necessary to put all the things we have shared so far into a plan. The plan should be simple, straightforward, and easy to implement. It should have the full support of the administration and middle level faculty. Over time, once all parts of the plan are in place, there should be an increase in the level of interest in reading for middle level students.

- Read Aloud—at least once a week, with all members of the school community serving as readers.

- Drop Everything and Read (DEAR)—fifteen minutes a day, every day, perhaps alternating classes, subject areas, or time periods, and all students should have a personal selection reading time as part of homework.

- Media Center Reading Environment—special area, special seating, display titles, advisory board of middle level students to help make ordering selections, review books, display new titles, include magazine rack with student-selected magazines, display of student-created books.

- Classroom Reading Environment—reading area with special seating, books available, attention to a wide variety of titles incorporated within all content areas, time to read, time to talk about books.

◀◀ School Community—all-school reading time, benches available for reading outside.

◀◀ Web Page—page for media center where students post reviews, and the media specialist can introduce new titles, promotions, general information, lists of links of interest to young adults.

◀◀ TV Production Studio—shows, panel discussions on books, information on authors, trivia games/contests.

◀◀ Publishing Center—where writers can produce books for peers and younger students.

◀◀ Book Clubs—for teachers to read and discuss YA literature, for students to get together to all read one title or one author or on one subject and then share ideas and thoughts on their readings, for parents, students, grade levels, etc.

◀◀ Curriculum Changes—to include literature in all content areas, encouraging all content area teachers to teach reading strategies, to allow students time to read.

◀◀ More Curriculum Changes—to help traditional English literature teachers include YA fiction to compare and contrast with classics, to emphasize students responding to literature on a personal level through literature circles and response journals, to explore reading workshop where students select their own reading material and work at their own pace, and where skill teaching is done on an as-needed basis.

◀◀ Visual Literacy—students should be taught to gather information and construct their own charts, graphs and diagrams; they need instruction in organizing large amounts of information—with special training in the use of a wide variety of graphic organizers—students also need to be taught skimming, scanning, note taking, and summarizing.

◀◀ Information Literacy—a research process like Big Six® should be taught and tied to the curriculum; library media specialists, computer teachers, and classroom teachers must work together to develop units and lessons that will include computer skills, information skills, and content-area curriculum outcomes.

◀◀ Special Events—connecting music and literature with plays, meaningful field trips, older students reading to and writing for younger students and vice-versa, author and illustrator visits.

◀◀ Booktalks—librarians, teachers, and students all sharing a brief and tantalizing glimpse of excellent titles to promote reading.

◀◀ Professional Development—sending teachers to reading conferences and workshops, opportunities to visit schools and libraries with good teen reading programs, memberships in professional reading organizations, professional libraries with lots of good books on reading, and professional journals for reading and discussion at faculty meetings.

◀◀ State-Sponsored Reading Programs—Florida has Sunshine State Readers, where students read from a short list and vote on their favorite titles.

◄◄ Bookshare—circulation of used books—kids bring in old books and buy back others for 50 cents each, teachers can have copies for classroom libraries, and the leftovers can be donated to local charities.

◄◄ Free Shelves—used books for students and teachers to take and replace with one of their own.

◄◄ Audio Books, Magazines, and Graphic Novels—should be part of a library collection for young adults.

In conclusion, the International Reading Association states that adolescents deserve

1. access to a wide variety of reading material that they can and want to read,

2. instruction that builds both the skill and desire to read increasingly complex materials,

3. assessment that shows them their strengths as well as their needs and that guides their teachers to design instruction that will best help them grow as readers,

4. expert teachers who model and provide explicit instruction in reading comprehension and study strategies across the curriculum,

5. reading specialists who assist individual students having difficulty learning how to read,

6. teachers who understand the complexities of individual adolescent readers, respect their differences, and respond to their characteristics, and

7. homes, communities, and a nation that will support their efforts to achieve advanced levels of literacy and provide the support necessary for them to succeed.

—Moore, D., T. Bean, D. Birdyshaw, and J. Rycik. *Adolescent Literacy: A Position Statement from the Commission on Adolescent Literacy.* International Reading Association, 1997.

A

Bibliography of Annotated Young Adult Titles

Abelove, Joan. *Go and Come Back.* DK Publishing Incorporated, 1998.

Anderson, Laurie Halse. *Speak.* Farrar Straus and Giroux, 1999.

———. *Fever 1793.* Simon & Schuster Books for Young Readers, 2000.

Bauer, Joan. *Squashed.* Delacorte Press, 1992.

———. *Rules of the Road.* G. P. Putnam's Sons, 1998.

———. *Backwater.* Putnam Publishing Group, 1999.

Billingsley, Franny. *The Folk Keeper.* Atheneum Books for Young Readers, 1999.

Block, Francesca Lia. *Violet & Claire.* HarperCollins Children's Book Group, 1999.

Bodett, Tom. *Williwaw!* Alfred A. Knopf, 1999.

Calabro, Marian. *The Perilous Journey of the Donner Party.* Clarion Books, 1999.

Cart, Michael, comp. *Tomorrowland: Ten Stories about the Future.* Scholastic Press, 1999.

Cooper, Susan. *King of Shadows.* Margaret K. McElderry Books, 1999.

Cormier, Robert. *Frenchtown Summer.* Delacorte Press, 1999.

Crew, Linda. *Children of the River.* Delacorte Press, 1989.

DeClements, Barthe. *Liar, Liar.* Marshall Cavendish, 1998.

Farmer, Nancy. *A Girl Named Disaster.* Puffin Books, 1996.

Fletcher, Ralph. *Fig Pudding.* Houghton Mifflin Company, 1995.

Gantos, Jack. *Joey Pigza Swallowed the Key.* Farrar, Straus and Giroux, 1998.

Gee, Maurice. *The Fat Man.* Simon & Schuster Children's Publishing, 1997.

Glenn, Mel. *Foreign Exchange.* Morrow Junior Books, 1999.

Griffin, Adele. *The Other Shephards.* Hyperion Books for Children, 1998.

Gutman, Dan. *Honus & Me.* Avon Books, 1997.

Haddix, Margaret Peterson. *Leaving Fishers.* Aladdin Paperbacks, 1997.

———. *Among the Hidden.* Simon & Schuster Books for Young Readers, 1998.

Holt, Kimberly Willis. *My Louisiana Sky.* Henry Holt and Company, 1998.

Howe, James. *The Watcher.* Aladdin Paperbacks, 1997.

Jimenez, Francisco. *Circuits: Stories from the Life of a Migrant Child.* University of New Mexico Press, 1997.

Jones, Diana Wynne. *Dark Lord of Derkholm.* Greenwillow Books, 1998.

Jordan, Sherryl. *The Raging Quiet.* Simon & Schuster Books for Young Readers, 1999.

Krisher, Trudy. *Spite Fences.* Laurel-Leaf Books, 1994.

LaFaye, A. *The Year of the Sawdust Man.* Simon & Schuster Books for Young Readers, 1998.

Lasky, Kathryn. *Elizabeth I, Red Rose of the House of Tudor.* Scholastic Incorporated, 1996.

Lerangis, Peter. *Antarctica: Journey to the Pole.* Scholastic Incorporated, 2000.

Levitin, Sonia. *The Cure.* Silver Whistle, 1999.

Matas, Carol, and Perry Nodelman. *Of Two Minds.* Simon & Schuster Books for Young Readers, 1995.

Matcheck, Diane. *The Sacrifice.* Farrar Straus and Giroux, 1998.

McCaughrean, Geraldine. *The Pirate's Son.* Scholastic Incorporated, 1996.

McKinley, Robin. *Spindle's End.* G. P. Putnam's Sons, 2000.

McNeal, Laura and Tom. *Crooked.* Alfred A. Knopf, 1999.

Metzger, Lois. *Missing Girls.* Viking Press, 1999.

Mikaelsen, Ben. *Petey.* Hyperion Books for Children, 1998.

Myers, Walter Dean. *At Her Majesty's Request: An African Princess in Victorian England.* Scholastic Incorporated, 1999.

———. *Monster.* Harper Collins Children's Book Group, 1999.

Namioka, Lensey. *Ties That Bind, Ties That Break.* Delacorte Press, 1999.

Napoli, Donna Jo. *Zel.* Dutton Children's Books, 1996.

Nix, Garth. *Shade's Children.* HarperCollins Children's Book Group, 1997.

Nixon, Joan Lowry. *Search for The Shadowman.* Delacorte Press, 1996.

Nolan, Han. *Dancing on the Edge.* Harcourt Brace, 1997.

Opdyke, Irene Gut. *In My Hands: Memories of a Holocaust Rescuer.* Alfred A. Knopf, 1999.

Paterson, Katherine. *Preacher's Boy.* Clarion Books, 1999.

Paulsen, Gary. *The Schernoff Discoveries.* Delacorte Press, 1997.

———. *Soldiers Heart.* Delacorte Press, 1998.

Randle, Kristen D. *Breaking Rank.* Morrow Junior Books, 1999.

Rennison, Louise. *Angus, Thongs and Full-Frontal Snogging: Confessions of Georgia Nicolson.* HarperCollins Children's Book Group, 2000.

Rinaldi, Ann. *Amelia's War.* Scholastic Press, 1999.

Ritter, John H. *Choosing Up Sides.* Philomel Books, 1998.

Roberts, Willo Davis. *The Kidnappers: A Mystery.* Atheneum Books for Young Readers, 1998.

Rowling, J. K. *Harry Potter and the Prisoner of Azkaban.* Scholastic Incorporated, 2000.

Sacher, Louis. *Holes.* Farrar, Straus and Giroux, 1998.

Shusterman, Neal. *Downsiders: A Novel.* Simon & Schuster Books for Young Readers, 1999.

Sleator, William. *The Boxes.* Dutton Children's Books, 1998.

———. *Rewind.* Dutton Children's Books, 1999.

Smith, Roland. *Jaguar.* Hyperion Books for Children, 1997.

Sones, Sonya. *Stop Pretending: What Happened When My Big Sister Went Crazy.* Harper-Collins, 1999.

Spinelli, Jerry. *Crash.* Alfred A. Knopf, 1996.

Springer, Nancy. *I Am Mordred: A Tale from Camelot.* Philomel Books, 1998.

Stanlely, Diane. *A Time Apart.* Morrow Junior Books, 1999.

Strasser, Todd. *The Wave.* Laurel-Leaf Books, 1981.

Tarbox, Katherine. *Katie.Com.* Dutton Children's Books, 2000.

Thomas, Jane Resh. *Behind the Mask: The Life of Queen Elizabeth I.* Clarion Books, 1998.

Williams, Laura E. *The Spider's Web.* Milkweed Editions, 1999.

Wilson, Diane Lee. *I Rode a Horse of Milk White Jade.* Orchard Books, 1998.

Woodson, Jacqueline. *If You Come Softly.* Puffin Books, 1998.

Wynne-Jones, Tim. *The Maestro.* Orchard Books, 1996.

————. *Stephen Fair.* DK Publishing, 1998.

————. *Lord of the Fries and Other Stories.* DK Publishing, 1999.

Yolen, Jane, and Bruce Coville. *Armageddon Summer.* Harcourt Brace, 1998.

Young, Karen Romano. *The Beetle and Me: A Love Story.* William Morrow and Company, 1999.

Zindel, Paul. *Rats.* Hyperion Books for Children, 1999.

B

Bibliography
of Professional Titles

Adamson, Lynda. *Literature Connections to World History Grades 7-12*. Libraries Unlimited, 1998.

Allen, Janet, and Kyle Gonzalez. *There's Room for Me Here: Literacy Workshop in the Middle School*. Stenhouse Publishers, 1998.

Ammon, Bette D., and Gale W. Sherman. *Worth a Thousand Words: An Annotated Guide to Picture Books for Older Readers*. Libraries Unlimited, 1996.

———. *More Rip-Roaring Reads for Reluctant Teen Readers*. Libraries Unlimited, 1998.

Atwell, Nancie. *In the Middle: New Understandings about Writing, Reading, and Learning*. Heinemann, 1998.

Barrett, Susan. *It's All in Your Head: A Guide to Understanding Your Brain and Boosting Your Brain Power*. Free Spirit, 1992.

Bauermeister, Erica, and Holly Smith. *Let's Hear It for the Girls: 375 Great Books for Readers 2-14*. Penguin, 1997.

Beers, Kylene, and Barbara Samuels, eds. *Into Focus: Understanding and Creating Middle School Readers*. Christopher-Gordon, 1998.

Benedict, Susan, and Lenore Carlisle, eds. *Beyond Words: Picture Books for Older Readers and Writers*. Heinemann, 1992.

Benjamin, A. *An English Teacher's Guide to Performance Tasks and Rubrics: Middle School*. Eye on Education, 2000.

Berman, Matt. *What Else Should I Read? Guiding Kids to Good Books*, vol. 2. Libraries Unlimited, 1996.

Billmeyer, Rachel, and Mary Lee Barton. *Teaching Reading in the Content Areas: If Not Me, Then Who?* McREL, 1998.

Blass, Rosanne, and Nancy Allen. *Responding to Literature: Activities for Grades 6, 7, 8.* Teacher Ideas Press, 1991.

Bodart, J., ed. *The New Booktalker,* vol. 1. Libraries Unlimited, 1992.

Booth, David. *Guiding the Reading Process: Techniques and Strategies for Successful Instruction in K-8 Classrooms.* Pembroke, 1998.

———, ed. *Literacy Techniques for Building Successful Readers and Writers.* Pembroke, 1996.

Borasi, Raffaella, and Marjorie Siegel. *Reading Counts: Expanding the Role of Reading in Mathematics Classrooms.* Teachers College Press, 2000.

Bromley, Karen, Linda DeVitis, and Marcia Modio. *50 Graphic Organizers for Reading, Writing & More.* Scholastic Professional Books, 1999.

Bullock, Richard, ed. *Why Workshop? Changing Course in 7-12 English.* Stenhouse Publishers, 1998.

Calkins, Lucy. *The Art of Teaching Reading.* Addison-Wesley Longman, 2001.

Chatton, B., and N. L. Collins. *Blurring the Edges: Integrated Curriculum through Writing and Children's Literature.* Heinemann, 1999.

Daniels, Harvey. *Literature Circles: Voice and Choice in the Student-Centered Classroom.* Stenhouse Publishers, 1994.

Dodson, Shireen. *100 Books for Girls to Grow On.* HarperCollins, 1998.

Drew, Bernard. *The 100 Most Popular Young Adult Authors: Biographical Sketches and Bibliographies.* Libraries Unlimited, 1997.

Ellis, A. K., and C. Stuen. *The Interdisciplinary Curriculum.* Eye on Education, 1998.

Flynn, Kris. *Graphic Organizers . . . Helping Children Think Visually.* Creative Teaching Press, 1995.

Forte, Imogene, and Sandra Schurr. *Graphic Organizers & Planning Outlines for Instruction and Assessment.* Incentive Publications, 1996.

Gambrell, Linda, and Janice Almasi, eds. *Lively Discussions! Fostering Engaged Reading.* International Reading Association, 1996.

Harvey, Stephanie. *Nonfiction Matters: Reading, Writing, and Research in Grades 3-8.* Stenhouse Publishers, 1998.

Harvey, Stephanie, and Anne Goudvis. *Strategies That Work: Teaching Comprehension to Enhance Understanding.* Stenhouse Publishers, 2000.

Herald, Diana. *Teen Genreflecting.* Libraries Unlimited, 1997.

Hersch, Patricia. *A Tribe Apart: A Journey into the Heart of American Adolescence.* Ballantine, 1998.

Herz, S. *From Hinton to Hamlet: Building Bridges between Young Adult Literature and the Classics.* Greenwood Press, 1996.

Hetzel, June. *Responding to Literature: Activities to Use with Any Literature Selection.* Creative Teaching Press, 1993.

Hurst, Carol Otis, and Rebecca Otis. *Using Literature in the Middle School Curriculum.* Linworth, 1999.

Hurst, Carol Otis, Lynn Otis Palmer, Vaughn Churchill, Margaret Sullivan Ahern, and Bernard G. McMahon. *Curriculum Connections: Picture Books in Grade 3 and Up.* Linworth, 1999.

International Society for Technology in Education. *National Educational Technology Standards for Students.* ISTE, 2000.

Jackson, Norma, with Paula Pillow. *The Reading-Writing Workshop: Getting Started.* Scholastic Professional Books, 1992.

Jensen, Eric. *Completing the Puzzle: The Brain-Compatible Approach to Learning—A Research-Based Guide to Implementing the Dramatic New Learning Paradigms.* The Brain Store, 1997.

———. *Introduction to Brain-Compatible Learning.* The Brain Store, 1998.

———. *Teaching with the Brain in Mind.* Association for Supervision and Curriculum Development, 1998.

Jody, Marilyn, and Marianne Saccardi. *Using Computers to Teach Literature: A Teacher's Guide.* National Council of Teachers of English, 1998.

Kaywell, Joan, ed. *Adolescent Literature as a Complement to the Classics, Volume 4.* Christopher-Gordon, 2000.

Knowles, Elizabeth, and Martha Smith. *The Reading Connection: Bringing Parents, Teachers, and Librarians Together.* Libraries Unlimited, 1997.

———. *More Reading Connections: Bringing Parents, Teachers, and Librarians Together.* Libraries Unlimited, 1999.

Langer, Judith. *Envisioning Literature: Literary Understanding and Literature Instruction.* Teachers College Press, 1995.

Leonhardt, Mary. *Keeping Kids Reading: How to Raise Avid Readers in the Video Age.* Three Rivers Press, 1996.

Littlejohn, Carol. *Talk That Book: Booktalks to Promote Reading.* Linworth, 1999.

———. *Keep Talking That Book! Booktalks to Promote Reading,* vol. 2. Linworth, 2000.

McElmeel, Sharron. *The Latest and Greatest Read-Alouds.* Libraries Unlimited, 1994.

———. *Great New Nonfiction Reads.* Libraries Unlimited, 1995.

McElmeel, S., and C. Smallwood. *WWW Almanac: Making Curriculum Connections to Special Days, Weeks, and Months.* Linworth, 1999.

Miller, Wilma. *Ready-to-Use Activities and Materials for Improving Content Reading Skills.* Prentice-Hall, 1999.

Moeller, M. and V. *Middle School English Teacher's Guide to Active Learning.* Eye on Education, 2000.

Morrow, Lesley Mandel. *The Literacy Center.* Stenhouse Publishers, 1997.

Moss, Joy. *Using Literature in the Middle Grades: A Thematic Approach.* Christopher-Gordon, 1994.

————. *Teaching Literature in the Middle Grades: A Thematic Approach.* Christopher-Gordon, 2000.

Muschla, G. *Reading Workshop Survival Kit.* Center for Applied Research in Education, 1997.

Neaman, Mimi, and Mary Strong. *Literature Circles: Cooperative Learning for Grades 3-8.* Teacher Ideas Press, 1992.

Noe, Katherine L. Schlick, and Nancy J. Johnson. *Getting Started with Literature Circles.* Christopher-Gordon Publishers, 1999.

Odean, Kathleen. *Great Books for Girls: More Than 600 Books to Inspire Today's Girls and Tomorrow's Women.* Ballantine Books, 1997.

Parsons, Les. *Response Journals.* Heinemann, 1990.

Pennac, Daniel. *Better Than Life.* Stenhouse/Pembroke, 1999.

Peterson, Ralph, and Maryann Eeds. *Grand Conversations: Literature Groups in Action.* Scholastic, 1990.

Purves, Alan, Theresa Rogers, and Anna Soter. *How Porcupines Make Love III: Readers, Texts, Cultures in The Response-Based Literature Classroom.* Longman, 1995.

Raphael, T., L. Pardo, K. Highfield, and S. McMahon. *Book Club: A Literature-Based Curriculum.* Small Planet Communications, 1997.

Reuter, Janet. *Creative Teaching Through Picture Books for Middle School Students.* Frank Schaffer, 1993.

Rief, Linda. *Vision and Voice: Extending the Literacy Spectrum.* Heinemann, 1999.

Roberts, Patricia, and Richard Kellough. *A Guide for Developing Interdisciplinary Thematic Units.* Prentice-Hall/Merrill, 2000.

Rosenblatt, Louise. *The Reader, the Text, the Poem: The Transactional Theory of the Literary Work.* Southern Illinois University Press, 1978.

Roser, Nancy, and Miriam Martinez, eds. *Book Talk and Beyond: Children and Teachers Respond to Literature.* International Reading Association, 1995.

Routman, Regie. *Conversations: Strategies for Teaching, Learning, and Evaluating.* Heinemann, 2000.

Ryan, Connie. *Hooked on Books: A Genre-Based Guide for 30 Adolescent Books.* Frank Schaffer, 1993.

Saunders, Sheryl Lee. *Look and Learn! Using Picture Books in Grades Five through Eight.* Heinemann, 1999.

Sheppard, Ronnie, and Beverly Stratton. *Reflections on Becoming: Fifteen Literature-Based Units for the Young Adolescent.* National Middle School Association, 1993.

Simmons, John, and Lawrence Baines. *Language Study in Middle School, High School, and Beyond: Views on Enhancing the Study of Language.* International Reading Association, 1998.

Soter, Anna. *Young Adult Literature and the New Library Theories: Developing Critical Readers in the Middle School.* Teachers College Press, 2000.

Sousa, David. *How the Brain Learns: A Classroom Teacher's Guide.* National Association of Secondary School Principals, 1995.

Spencer, P. *What Do Young Adults Read Next? A Reader's Guide to Fiction for Young Adults.* Gale Research, 1994.

———. *What Do Young Adults Read Next? Volume Two: A Reader's Guide to Fiction for Young Adults.* Gale Research, 1997.

Sprenger, Marilee. *Learning & Memory: The Brain in Action.* Association for Supervision and Curriculum Development, 1999.

Stoll, Donald, ed. *Magazines for Kids and Teens.* International Reading Association, 1997.

Sylwester, Robert. *A Celebration of Neurons: An Educator's Guide to the Human Brain.* Association for Supervision and Curriculum Development, 1995.

Vacca, Richard, and JoAnne Vacca. *Content Area Reading: Literacy and Learning Across the Curriculum.* Addison-Wesley Longman, 1999.

Wadham, Tim and Rachel. *Bringing Fantasy Alive for Children and Young Adults.* Linworth, 1999.

Whitfield, Jamie. *Getting Kids Hooked on Literature: A Hands-On Guide to Making Literature Exciting for Kids.* Prufrock Press, 1998.

Wilhelm, Jeffrey. *You've Gotta BE the Book: Teaching Engaged and Reflective Reading with Adolescents.* Teachers College Press, 1995.

Wollman-Bonilla, Julie. *Response Journals.* Scholastic Professional Books, 1992.

C

Award-Winning Books

∽ Michael L. Printz Award

The Michael L. Printz Award is given for the book that exemplifies literary excellence in young adult literature. It is named for a Topeka, Kansas, school librarian who was a long-time active member of the Young Adult Library Services Association.

◂◂ 2001 Award Winner

Almond, David. *Kit's Wilderness*. Delecorte, 1999.

◂◂ 2001 Honor Books

Coman, Carolyn. *Many Stones*. Front Street, 2000.

Plum-Ucci, Carol. *The Body of Christopher Creed*. Harcourt Brace, 2000.

Rennison, Louise. *Angus, Thongs, and Full Frontal Snogging: Confessions of Georgia Nicolson*. HarperCollins, 2000.

Trueman, Terry. *Stuck in Neutral*. HarperCollins, 1999.

◂◂ 2000 Award Winner

Myers, Walter Dean. *Monster*. HarperCollins, 1999.

◂◂ 2000 Honor Books

Almond, David. *Skellig*. Delacorte Press, 1999.

Anderson, Laurie Halse. *Speak*. Farrar, Straus and Giroux, 1999.

Wittlinger, Ellen. *Hard Love*. Simon & Schuster Books for Young Readers, 1999.

◠ *Newbery Medal*

John Newbery (1713-1766) was a British printer and bookseller, who first began publishing books for children. This award was established in 1922 and is presented to the author of the best book published for children in the preceding year.

◂◂ 2001 Award Winner

Peck, Richard. *A Year Down Yonder*. Dial Books for Young Readers, 1999.

◂◂ 2001 Honor Books

DiCamillo, Kate. *Because of Winn-Dixie*. Candlewick Press, 2000.
Bauer, Joan. *Hope Was Here*. G. P. Putnam's Sons, 2000.
Gantos, Jack. *Joey Pigza Loses Control*. Farrar, Straus and Giroux, 2000.
Creech, Sharon. *The Wanderer*. HarperCollins Children's Book Group, 2000.

◂◂ 2000 Award Winner

Curtis, Christopher Paul. *Bud, Not Buddy*. Delacorte Press, 1999.

◂◂ 2000 Honor Books

Couloumbis, Audrey. *Getting Near to Baby*. Capricorn Books, 1999.
dePaola, Tomie. *26 Fairmount Avenue*. Putnam Publishing Group, 1999.
Holm, Jennifer L. *Our Only May Amelia*. HarperCollins Children's Book Group, 1999.

◂◂ 1999 Award Winner

Sachar, Louis. *Holes*. Farrar, Straus and Giroux, 1998.

◂◂ 1998 Award Winner

Hesse, Karen. *Out of the Dust*. Scholastic Press, 1997.

◂◂ 1997 Award Winner

Konigsburg, E. L. *The View from Saturday*. Atheneum Books for Young Readers, 1996.

◂◂ 1996 Award Winner

Cushman, Karen. *The Midwife's Apprentice*. Clarion Books, 1995.

◀ 1995 Award Winner

Creech, Sharon. *Walk Two Moons*. HarperCollins Children's Book Group, 1994.

◁ *The Coretta Scott King Award*

This award commemorates Dr. Martin Luther King Jr. and honors his wife, Coretta Scott King, for her continued work for brotherhood and world peace. The award is made to one black author, and since 1974, to one black illustrator. Their works must be educational as well as inspirational.

◀ 2001 Award Winner—Text

Woodson, Jaquelin. *Miracle's Boys.* G. P. Putnam's Sons, 1999.

◀ 2001 Award Winner—Illustrator

Collier Bryan. *Uptown*. Henry Holt and Company, 2000.

◀ 2000 Award Winner—Text

Curtis, Christopher Paul. *Bud, Not Buddy.* Delacorte Press, 1999.

◀ 2000 Honor Books

English, Karen. *Francie.* Farrar, Straus and Giroux, 1999.
McKissack, Patricia C. and Frederick. *Black Hands, White Sails: The Story of African-American Whalers.* Scholastic Incorporated, 1999.
Myers, Walter Dean. *Monster.* HarperCollins Children's Book Group, 1999.

◀ 2000 Award Winner—Illustrator

Pinkney, Brian. *In the Time of the Drums.* Hyperion Books for Children, 1999 (text by Kim Seigelson).

◀ 2000 Honor Books

Lewis, E. B. *My Rows and Piles of Coins.* Houghton Mifflin Company, 1999 (text by Tololwa M. Mollel).
Myers, Christopher. *Black Cat.* Scholastic Incorporated, 1999.

◀ 1999 Award Winner—Text

Johnson, Angela. *Heaven.* Simon & Schuster Books for Young Readers, 1998.

◂◂ 1999 Award Winner—Illustrator

Wood, Michele. *I See the Rhythm*. Children's Book Press, 1998 (text by Toyomi Igus).

◂◂ 1998 Award Winner—Text

Draper, Sharon M. *Forged by Fire*. Atheneum Books for Young Readers, 1997.

◂◂ 1998 Award Winner—Illustrator

Steptoe, Javaka. *In Daddy's Arms I Am Tall: African Americans Celebrating Fathers*. Lee & Low, 1997.

◂◂ 1997 Award Winner—Text

Myers, Walter Dean. *Slam*. Scholastic Incorporated, 1996.

◂◂ 1997 Award Winner—Illustrator

Pinkney, Jerry. *Minty: A Story of Young Harriet Tubman*. Dial Books for Young Readers, 1996 (text by Alan Schroeder).

◂◂ 1996 Award Winner—Text

Hamilton, Virginia. *Her Stories*. Blue Sky Press, 1995.

◂◂ 1996 Award Winner—Illustrator

Feelings, Tom. *The Middle Passage: White Ships Black Cargo*. Dial Books for Young Readers, 1995.

◂◂ 1995 Award Winner—Text

McKissack, Patricia and Frederick. *Christmas in the Big House, Christmas in the Quarters*. Scholastic Incorporated, 1994.

◂◂ 1995 Award Winner—Illustrator

Ransome, James. *The Creation*. Holiday House, 1994 (text by James Weldon Johnson).

ᴄᴡ *The Mildred L. Batchelder Award*

This award, established in 1966, is offered by the Association for Library Service to Children, a division of the American Library Association. The award is given to an American publisher for a children's book originally published in a foreign language. It is usually awarded at the ALS midwinter meeting unless the committee feels there is no worthy recipient for that year.

◂◂ 2001 Award Winner

Carmi, Daniella. *Samir and Yonatan*. Scholastic Incorporated, 1999. Translated from the Hebrew by Yael Lotan.

◂◂ 2000 Award Winner

Quintana, Anton. *The Baboon King*. Walker & Company, 1999.

◂◂ 1999 Award Winner

Rabinovici, Schoschana. *Thanks to My Mother*. Dial Books for Young Readers, 1998. Edited by Cindy Kane, translated from the Hebrew by James Skofield.

◂◂ 1998 Award Winner

Holub, Josef. *The Robber and Me*. Henry Holt & Company, 1997. Edited by Marc Aronson and translated from the German by Elizabeth D. Crawford.

◂◂ 1997 Award Winner

Kazumi, Yumoto. *The Friends*. Farrar, Straus and Giroux, 1996. Translated from the Japanese by Cathy Hirano.

◂◂ 1996 Award Winner

Orlev, Uri. *The Lady with the Hat*. Houghton Mifflin Company, 1995. Translated from the Hebrew by Hillel Hilkin.

◂◂ 1995 Award Winner

Reuter, Bjarne. *The Boys from St. Petri*. Dutton Children's Books, 1994. Translated from the Danish by Anthea Bell.

❧ *Margaret A. Edwards Award for Outstanding Literature for Young Adults*

Margaret A. Edwards promoted young adult literature and services at the Enoch Pratt Free Library for over 30 years. This award was established in 1988 and honors a young adult author for his or her lifetime achievement.

◂◂ 2001 Award Winner—Robert Lipsyte

◂◂ 2000 Award Winner—Chris Crutcher

◂ 1999 Award Winner—Anne McCaffrey

◂ 1998 Award Winner—Madeleine L'Engle

◂ 1997 Award Winner—Gary Paulsen

◂ 1996 Award Winner—Judy Blume

◂ 1995 Award Winner—Cynthia Voigt

◂ 1994 Award Winner—Walter Dean Myers

◂ 1993 Award Winner—M. E. Kerr

◂ 1992 Award Winner—Lois Duncan

◂ 1991 Award Winner—Robert Cormier

◂ 1990 Award Winner—Richard Peck

∾ Boston Globe-Horn Book Awards

The *Boston Globe* newspaper and *Horn Book Magazine* established this award in 1967. Each year, three awards are given: one for illustrator, one for fiction or poetry, and one for nonfiction.

◂ 2000 Fiction Award Winner

Billingsley, Franny. *The Folk Keeper.* Atheneum Books for Young Readers, 1999.

◂ 2000 Nonfiction Award Winner

Aronson, Marc. *Sir Walter Raleigh & the Quest for El Dorado.* Houghton Mifflin Company, 2000.

◂ 1999 Fiction Award Winner

Sachar, Louis. *Holes.* Farrar, Straus and Giroux, 1998.

◂ 1999 Nonfiction Award Winner

Jenkins, Steve. *The Top of the World: Climbing Mount Everest.* Houghton Mifflin Company, 1999.

◂ 1999 Special Citation

Sis, Peter. *Tibet: Through the Red Box.* Farrar, Straus and Giroux, 1998.

◂ 1998 Fiction Award Winner

Jimenez, Francisco. *Circuits: Stories from the Life of a Migrant Child.* University of New Mexico Press, 1997.

◄◄ 1998 Nonfiction Award Winner

Tillage, Leon. *Leon's Story*. Farrar, Straus and Giroux, 1997.

◄◄ 1997 Fiction Award Winner

Yumoto, Kazumi. *The Friends*. Farrar, Straus and Giroux, 1996.

◄◄ 1997 Nonfiction Award Winner

Wick, Walter. *A Drop of Water: A Book of Science and Wonder*. Scholastic Incorporated, 1997.

◄◄ 1996 Fiction Award Winner

Avi. *Poppy*. Orchard Books, 1995.

◄◄ 1996 Nonfiction Award Winner

Warren, Andrea. *Orphan Train Rider: One Boy's True Story*. Houghton Mifflin Company, 1996.

◄◄ 1995 Fiction Award Winner

Wynne-Jones, Tim. *Some of the Kinder Planets*. Orchard Books, 1995.

◄◄ 1995 Nonfiction Award Winner

Bober, Natalie S. *Abigail Adams: Witness to a Revolution*. Atheneum Books for Young Readers, 1995.

∾ The National Book Award for Young People's Literature

The National Book Foundation recognizes a book of literary merit written for children or young adults by an American writer. The young adult category was added in 1996, and books of all genres are considered.

◄◄ 2000 Award Winner

Whelan Gloria. *Homeless Bird*. HarperCollins Publishers, 2000.

◄◄ 1999 Award Winner

Holt, Kimberly Willis. *When Zachary Beaver Came to Town*. Henry Holt and Company, 1999.

◄◄ 1998 Award Winner

Sachar, Louis. *Holes*. Farrar, Straus and Giroux, 1998.

◀ 1997 Award Winner

Nolan, Han. *Dancing on the Edge*. Harcourt Brace Juvenile Books, 1997.

◀ 1996 Award Winner

Martinez, Victor. *Parrot in the Oven: Mi Vida*. HarperCollins Children's Book Group, 1996.

⌒ *American Booksellers Book of the Year— Children's Prize*

The ABBY awards are given each year by the ABA bookstore members for adult and children's books they enjoyed recommending throughout the year to their customers.

◀ 1999 Award Winner

Rowling, J. K. *Harry Potter and the Sorcerer's Stone.* Scholastic Incorporated, 1999.

◀ 1998 Award Winner

Brett, Jan. *The Hat.* Penguin Putnam Books for Young Readers, 1997.

◀ 1998—YA Nominee

Hest, Amy. *When Jessie Came Across the Sea*. Candlewick Press, 1997.

◀ 1997 Award Winner

Henkes, Kevin. *Lilly's Purple Plastic Purse*. Greenwillow Books, 1996.

◀ 1997 YA Nominees

Pullman, Philip. *The Golden Compass*. Alfred A. Knopf, 1996.
Silverstein, Shel. *Falling Up*. HarperCollins Children's Book Group, 1996.

◀ 1996 Award Winner

McBratney, Sam. *Guess How Much I Love You.* Candlewick Press, 1995.

◀ 1996 YA Nominee

Cushman, Karen. *Catherine Called Birdy.* Houghton Mifflin Company, 1994.

◀ 1995 Award Winner

Pfister, Marcus. *Rainbow Fish*. North-South Books, 1992.

◂◂ 1995 YA Nominees

Lowry, Lois. *The Giver*. Houghton Mifflin Company, 1993.

Polacco, Patricia. *Pink and Say*. Philomel Books, 1994.

∾ *The Christopher Awards—Books for Young People*

Films, broadcast TV and cable programs, and books for adults and young people are recognized for their ability to "affirm the highest values of the human spirit." They remind audiences and readers of the impact of the media and its ability to positively affect and shape our world.

◂◂ 2001 Award Winners

Pomerantz, Charlotte. *The Mousery*. Harcourt Children's Books, 1999 (ages 9-10).

Deedy, Carmen Agra. *The Yellow Star*. Peachtree Publishers, Ltd., 2000 (ages 11-12).

Bauer, Joan. *Hope Was Here*. G. P. Putnam's Sons, 2000.

Creech, Sharon. *The Wanderer*. HarperCollins Children's Book Group, 2000 (YA).

◂◂ 2000 Award Winners

Borden, Louise. *Good Luck, Mrs. K.* Margaret K. McElderry, 1999 (ages 8-10).

Schuch, Steve. *A Symphony of Whales*. Harcourt Children's Books, 1999 (ages 10-12).

Sones, Sonya. *Stop Pretending: What Happened When My Big Sister Went Crazy*. HarperCollins Children's Book Group, 1999 (ages 12 and up).

Wood, Douglas. *Grandad's Prayers of the Earth*. Candlewick Press, 1999 (all ages).

◂◂ 1999 Award Winners

Brisson, Pat. *The Summer My Father Was Ten*. Boyds Mills Press, 1998 (ages 8-10).

Wells, Rosemary. *Mary on Horseback: Three Mountain Stories*. Dial Books for Young Readers, 1998 (ages 10-12).

Hill, Donna. *Shipwreck Season*. Clarion Books, 1998 (ages 12 and up).

Sachar, Louis. *Holes*. Farrar, Straus and Giroux, 1998 (YA).

◂◂ 1998 Award Winners

Hest, Amy. *When Jessie Came Across the Sea*. Candlewick Press, 1997 (ages 8-10).

Bonners, Susan. *The Silver Balloon.* Farrar, Straus and Giroux, 1997 (ages 10-12).

Bitton-Jackson, Livia. *I Have Lived a Thousand Years: Growing Up in the Holocaust.* Simon & Schuster Children's Publishing, 1997 (YA).

◄◄ 1997 Award Winners

Clements, Andrew. *Frindle.* Simon & Schuster Books for Young Readers, 1996 (ages 10-12).

Calvert, Patricia. *Glennis, Before and After.* Atheneum Books for Young Readers, 1996 (ages 12 and up).

Kuklin, Susan. *Irrepressible Spirit: Conversations with Human Rights Activists.* G. P. Putnam's Sons, 1996 (YA).

◄◄ 1996 Award Winners

Hopkins, Lee Bennett. *Been to Yesterdays: Poems of a Life.* Boyds Mills Press, 1995 (ages 10-12).

Kraft, Betsy Harvey. *Mother Jones: One Woman's Fight for Labor.* Houghton Mifflin Company, 1995 (ages 12-14).

Ayer, Eleanor. *Parallel Journeys.* Atheneum Books for Young Readers, 1995 (YA).

◄◄ 1995 Award Winners

Grutman, Jewel H., and Gay Matthaei. *The Ledgerbook of Thomas Blue Eagle.* Thomasson-Grant, Incorporated, 1994 (ages 8-12).

Alexander, Sally Hobart. *Taking Hold: My Journey into Blindness.* Macmillan Books for Young Readers, 1994 (ages 12 and up).

∼ Pura Belpre Award

Pura Belpre was the first Latin librarian at the New York Public Library. This award was established in 1996 and is presented to a Latino/Latin writer and illustrator whose work best portrays, affirms, and celebrates the Latino cultural experience in an outstanding work of literature for children and youth. It is cosponsored by the Association for Library Service to Children (ALSC), a division of the American Library Association (ALA) and the National Association to Promote Library Services to the Spanish Speaking (REFORMA), an ALA affiliate.

◄◄ 2000 Award Winners

Ada, Alma Flor. *Under the Royal Palms: A Childhood in Cuba.* Atheneum Books for Young Readers, 1998 (narrative).

Garza, Carmen Lomaz. *Magic Windows.* Children's Book Press, 1999 (illustrations).

◀◀ 1998 Award Winners

Martinez, Victor. *Parrot in the Oven: Mi Vida*. HarperCollins Children's Book Group, 1996 (narrative).

Soto, Gary. *Snapshots from the Wedding*, illustrated by Stephanie Garcia. G. P. Putnam's Sons, 1997 (illustrations).

◀◀ 1996 Award Winners

Cofer, Judith Ortiz. *An Island Like You: Stories of the Barrio*. Orchard Books, 1995 (narrative).

Soto, Gary. *Chato's Kitchen*. Illustrated by Susan Guevara. G. P. Putnam's Sons, 1995 (illustrations).

❧ Laura Ingalls Wilder Medal

Administered by the Association for Library Service to Children, a division of the American Library Association, the Ingalls Wilder Award was first given to its namesake in 1954. From 1960 to 1980, it was given every five years. Since 1983, this bronze medal has been given every three years to an author or illustrator who has made a long-lasting contribution to children's literature.

◀◀ 2001 Award Winner—Milton Meltzer

◀◀ 1998 Award Winner—Russell Freedman

◀◀ 1995 Award Winner—Virginia Hamilton

◀◀ 1992 Award Winner—Marcia Brown

◀◀ 1989 Award Winner—Elizabeth George Spear

◀◀ 1986 Award Winner—Jean Fritz

◀◀ 1983 Award Winner—Maurice Sendak

❧ The Golden Kite Award

Four Golden Kite Awards are given each year by the Society of Children's Book Writers and Illustrators. These awards are given to outstanding children's books published during the year by members of the society. The statuettes are awarded for fiction, nonfiction, picture book text, and picture-illustration.

◀◀ 1999 Award Winner—Fiction

Anderson, Laurie Halse. *Speak*. Farrar, Straus and Giroux, 1999.

◂◂ 1999 Award Winner—Nonfiction

Dyson, Marianne J. *Space Station Science: Life in Free Fall.* Scholastic Incorporated, 1999.

◂◂ 1998 Award Winner—Fiction

Bauer, Joan. *Rules of the Road.* G. P. Putnam's Sons, 1998.

◂◂ 1998 Award Winner—Nonfiction

Freedman, Russell. *Martha Graham: A Dancer's Life.* Clarion Books, 1997.

◂◂ 1997 Award Winner—Fiction

Napoli, Donna Jo. *Stones in the Water.* Dutton Children's Books, 1997.

◂◂ 1997 Award Winner—Nonfiction

Schulman, Arlene. *Carmine's Story: A Book About a Boy Living with AIDS.* Lerner Publishing, 1997.

◂◂ 1996 Award Winner—Fiction

McGraw, Eloise. *The Moorchild.* Margaret K. McElderry, 1996.

◂◂ 1996 Award Winner—Nonfiction

Kehret, Peg. *Small Steps*: *The Year I Got Polio.* Albert Whitman & Company, 1996.

◂◂ 1995 Award Winner—Fiction

Curtis, Christopher Paul. *The Watsons Go to Birmingham—1963.* Delacorte Press, 1995.

◂◂ 1995 Award Winner—Nonfiction

Bober, Natalie S. *Abigail Adams*: *Witness to a Revolution.* Atheneum Books for Young Readers, 1995.

❧ *The Orbis Pictus Award for Outstanding Nonfiction for Children*

This award is presented by the National Council of Teachers of English for promoting and recognizing excellence in nonfiction books for children. It is named after the first book written specifically for children, Orbis Pictus—The World in Pictures (1657) by Johannes Amos Comenius.

◂◂ 2000 Award Winner

Bridges, Ruby. *Through My Eyes*. Scholastic Press, 1999.

◂◂ 1999 Award Winner

Armstrong, Jennifer. *Shipwreck at the Bottom of the World: The Extraordinary True Story of Shackleton and the Endurance*. Crown Publishing Group, Incorporated, 1998.

◂◂ 1998 Award Winner

Pringle, Lawrence P. *Extraordinary Life.* Orchard Books, 1997.

◂◂ 1997 Award Winner

Stanlely, Diane. *Leonardo da Vinci*. William Morrow & Company, 1996.

◂◂ 1996 Award Winner

Murphy, Jim. *The Great Fire*. Scholastic Incorporated, 1995.

◂◂ 1995 Award Winner

Swanson, Diane. *Safari Beneath the Sea: The Wonder World of the North Pacific Coast*. Sierra Club Books for Children, 1996.

❧ Jane Addams Book Award: Children's Books That Build for Peace

Since 1953, this award has been given annually by the Women's International League for Peace and Freedom and the Jane Addams Peace Association. This book award is given each fall to an author who has world peace and social justice as a predominant theme.

◂◂ 2000 Award Winner

Bridges, Ruby. *Through My Eyes*. Scholastic Press, 1999.

◂◂ 1999 Award Winner

Wolff, Virginia Euwer. *Bat 6*. Scholastic Incorporated, 1998.

◂◂ 1998 Award Winner

Nye, Naomi Shihab. *Habibi.* Simon & Schuster Books for Young Readers, 1997.

◂◂ 1997 Award Winner

Bartoletti, Susan Campbell. *Growing Up in Coal Country*. Houghton Mifflin Company, 1996.

◂◂ 1996 Award Winner

Taylor, Mildred D. *The Well*. Dial Books for Young Readers, 1995.

◂◂ 1995 Award Winner

Freedman, Russell. *Kids at Work: Lewis Hine and the Crusade Against Child Labor*. Clarion Books, 1994.

∾ Giverny Book Award

The Giverny Award was established in 1998 and is given to the author and illustrator of a children's science picture book written in the English language in the past five years. The artwork, illustrations, photographs, or graphics along with the text must teach at least one scientific principle or encourage the young reader toward specific science-related pursuits or inquiry. If all other factors are equal, books about plants and/or plant science will have preference. The award is given by the 15 Degree Laboratory based at Louisiana State University.

◂◂ 2000 Award Winner

Pfeffer, Wendy. *A Log's Life*. Simon & Schuster Children's Publishing, 1997.

◂◂ 1999 Award Winner

Pety, Kate, and Axel Scheffler. *Sam Plants a Sunflower*. Macmillan Children's Books, 1997.

◂◂ 1998 Award Winner

Bang, Molly. *Common Ground: The Water, Earth, and Air We Share*. Blue Sky Press, 1997.

∾ Scott O'Dell Historical Fiction Award

Author Scott O'Dell (1898-1989) originated and donated this award for a distinguished work of historical fiction. Books to be considered must be published in English by a publisher in the United States. The setting of the book must be North, Central, or South America.

◂◂ 2000 Award Winner

Bat-Ami, Mirian. *Two Suns in the Sky*. Front Street Cricket Books, 1998.

◂◂ 1999 Award Winner

Robinet, Harriette Gillem. *Forty Acres and Maybe a Mule*. Atheneum Books for Young Readers, 1998.

◂◂ 1998 Award Winner

Hesse, Karen. *Out of the Dust*. Scholastic Incorporated, 1997.

◂◂ 1997 Award Winner

Paterson, Katherine. *Jip: His Story*. Lodestar Books, 1996.

◂◂ 1996 Award Winner

Taylor, Theodore. *The Bomb*. Harcourt Brace Juvenile Books, 1995.

◂◂ 1995 Award Winner

Salisbury, Graham. *Under the Blood Red Sun*. Delacorte Press, 1994.

❧ *The Edgar Awards*

These awards are presented annually by the Mystery Writers of America. They are named after their mentor, Edgar Allan Poe.

▣ Best YA Mystery

◂◂ 2000 Award Winner

Vande Velde, Vivian. *Never Trust a Dead Man*. Harcourt Brace Juvenile Books, 1999.

◂◂ 1999 Award Winner

Van Draanen, Wendelin. *Sammy Keyes and the Hotel Thief*. Alfred A. Knopf, 1998.

◂◂ 1998 Award Winner

Hobbs, Will. *Ghost Canoe*. William Morrow and Company, 1996.

◂◂ 1997 Award Winner

Roberts, Willo Davis. *Twisted Summer*. Atheneum Books for Young Readers, 1995.

◂◂ 1996 Award Winner

MacGregor, Rob. *Prophecy Rock*. Simon & Schuster Books for Young Readers, 1995.

▸ 1995 Award Winner

Springer, Nancy. *Toughing It.* Harcourt Brace Juvenile Books, 1994.

∽ *Hans Christian Andersen Medals*

The International Board on Books for Young People gives this award every two years to one living author and illustrator, at the time of the nomination. This medal is often called the Little Nobel Prize and is for an entire body of work.

▸ Author—Ana Maria Machado (Brazil) 2000

▸ Author—Katherine Paterson (United States) 1998

▸ Author—Uri Orlev (Israel) 1996

▸ Author—Michio Mado (Japan) 1994

▸ Author—Virginia Hamilton (United States) 1992

▸ Author—Tormod Haugen (Norway) 1990

∽ *Phoenix Award*

The Children's Literature Association annually recognizes books of high literary merit. These books were published in English originally and did not receive an award at the time of publication.

▸ 2000 Award Winner

Hughes, Monica. *The Keeper of the Isis Light.* Atheneum Books for Young Readers, 1998.

▸ 1999 Award Winner

Konigsburg, E. L. *Throwing Shadows.* Macmillan Publishing Company, 1988.

▸ 1998 Award Winner

Walsh, Jill Paton. *A Chance Child.* Morrow Avon, 1980.

▸ 1997 Award Winner

Cormier, Robert. *I Am the Cheese.* Bantam Doubleday Dell Books for Young Readers, 1991.

▸ 1996 Award Winner

Garner, Alan. *The Stone Book.* Chivers Audio Books, 1988.

◄◄ 1995 Award Winner

Yep, Laurence. *Dragonwings.* HarperCollins Children's Book Group, 1975.

∾ *The Mythopoeic Awards for Children's Literature*

This award is given to a fantasy book for young adults to picture books for beginning readers. The book must be published during the year it is nominated and written in the style of *The Hobbit* or *The Chronicles of Narnia.* Books from a series are eligible if they stand on their own, otherwise the series is eligible the year the final volume is published.

◄◄ 2000 Award Winner

Billingsley, Franny. *The Folk Keeper.* Atheneum Books for Young Readers, 1999.

◄◄ 1999 Award Winner

Jones, Diana Wynne. *Dark Lord of Derkholm.* HarperCollins Children's Book Group, 1998.

◄◄ 1998 Award Winner

Yolen, Jane. *Young Merlin Trilogy* (consisting of *Passager,* 1997; *Hobby,* 1996; and *Merlin,* 1997), Harcout Brace Juvenile Books.

◄◄ 1997 Award Winner

Windling, Terri. *The Wood Wife*. Tor Books, 1997.

◄◄ 1996 Award Winner

Jones, Diana Wynne. *The Crown of Dalemark.* HarperCollins Children's Book Group, 1995.

∾ *Sydney Taylor Book Awards*

This award is given by the Association of Jewish Libraries to a children's and young adult book of literary merit that reflect positive Jewish content and values.

▣ Young Adult Awards

◄◄ 2000 Award Winner

Vos, Ida. *The Key Is Lost*. William Morrow and Company, 1999.

◄◄ 1999 Award Winner

Rosen, Sybil. *Speed of Light.* Atheneum Books for Young Readers, 1999.

◂ 1998 Award Winner

Napoli, Donna Jo. *Stones in Water.* Dutton Children's Books, 1997.

◂ 1997 Award Winner

Jaffe, Nina. *The Mysterious Visitor: Stories of the Prophet Elijah.* Scholastic Incorporated, 1997.

◂ 1996 Award Winner

Schur, Maxine Rose. *When I Left My Village.* Dial Books for Young Readers, 1996.

◂ 1995 Award Winner

Vos, Ida. *Dancing on the Bridge of Avignon.* Houghton Mifflin Company, 1995.

❧ *Australian Children's Book of the Year Award*

This award was first established in 1946 and includes categories for picture books, younger readers, older readers, and in 2001, early childhood.

◂ 2000 Award Winner—Older Readers

Earls, Nick. *48 Shades of Brown.* Penguin Books, 1999.

◂ 1999 Award Winner—Older Readers

Gwynne, Phillip. *Deadly Unna?* Penguin Books, 1998.

◂ 1998 Award Winner—Older Readers

Jinks, Catherine. *Eye to Eye.* Puffin Books, 1998.

◂ 1997 Award Winner—Older Readers

Moloney, James. *A Bridge to Wiseman's Cove.* University of Queensland Press, 1997.

◂ 1996 Award Winner—Older Readers

Jinks, Catherine. *Pagan's Vows.* Omnibus Books, 1996.

∾ The Carnegie Medal

This is awarded by the Young Libraries Group of the British Library Association to an outstanding book written in English and published first, or concurrently, in the United Kingdom. The date reflects the year it was published, and the award is presented the following year.

◄◄ 1999 Award Winner

Chambers, Aidan. *Postcards from No Man's Land.* Bodley Head Children's Books Paperback, 1999.

◄◄ 1998 Award Winner

Almond, David. *Skellig.* Delacorte Press, 1999.

◄◄ 1997 Award Winner

Bowler, Tim. *River Boy*. Margaret K. McElderry, 2000.

◄◄ 1996 Award Winner

Burgess, Melvin. *Junk*. Methuen Publishing, 2000.

◄◄ 1995 Award Winner

Pullman, Philip. *Northern Lights*. U.S. title: *The Golden Compass*. Alfred A. Knopf, 1996.

∾ Information Book of the Year

This is awarded by the Children's Literature Roundtable of Canada for an information book published in Canada the previous year. It must be written in English by a Canadian citizen for children ages 5 through 15.

◄◄ 1999 Award Winner

Greenwood, Barbara. *The Last Safe House: The Story of the Underground Railroad.* Kids Can Press, 1998.

◄◄ 1998 Award Winner

Tanaka, Shelley. *The Buried City of Pompeii.* Hyperion Books for Children, 1997.

◄◄ 1997 Award Winner

Tanaka, Shelley. *On Board the Titanic*. Hyperion Books for Children, 1996.

◂ 1996 Award Winner

Granfield, Linda. *In Flanders Fields: The Story of the Poem by John McCrae*. Stoddart Publishing, 2000.

◂ 1995 Award Winner

Greenwood, Barbara. *A Pioneer Story: The Daily Life of a Canadian Family in 1840*. Kids Can Press, out of print.

∾ *Governor-General's Awards for Children's Literature*

This award for text was established in 1975, and the award for illustration in 1977. The award is given to the best book by a Canadian author, no matter where the book is published.

◂ 2000 Award Winner—Text

Ellis, Deborah. *Looking for X.* Groundwood Books, 2000.

◂ 2000 Award Winner—Illustration

Gay, Marie-Louise. *Yuck, A Love Story*. Stoddart Kids, 2000.

◂ 1999 Award Winner—Text

Gilmore, Rachna. *A Screaming Kind of Day.* Fitzhenny & Whiteside Ltd., 2000.

◂ 1999 Award Winner—Illustration

Clement, Gary. *The Great Poochini.* Groundwood Books, 1999.

◂ 1998 Award Winner—Text

Lunn, Janet. *The Hollow Tree.* Viking Penguin, 2000.

◂ 1998 Award Winner—Illustration

Denton, Kady MacDonald. *A Child's Treasury of Nursery Rhymes*. Larousse Kingfisher Chambers, 1998.

◂ 1997 Award Winner—Text

Pearson, Kit. *Awake and Dreaming. Viking* Penguin, 1997.

◂ 1997 Award Winner—Illustration

Reid, Barbara. *The Party*. Scholastic Incorporated, 1999.

◄◄ 1996 Award Winner—Text

Yee, Paul. *Ghost Train*. Publishers Group West, 1996.

◄◄ 1996 Award Winner—Illustration

Conrad, Pamo. *The Rooster's Gift*. Illustrated by Eric Beddows. HarperCollins Children's Book Group, 1996.

◄◄ 1995 Award Winner—Text

Wynne-Jones, Tim. *The Maestro.* Orchard Books, 1996.

◄◄ 1995 Award Winner—Illustration

Zeman, Ludmila. *The Last Quest of Gilgamesh*. Tundra Books of Northern New York, 1995.

∾ *Canadian Library Association Young Adult Book Award*

This award was established in 1980 for creative literature published in Canada. The creative work may be a novel, play, or poetry.

◄◄ 2000 Award Winner

Holubitsky, Katherine. *Alone at Ninety Foot.* Orca Book Publishers, 1999.

◄◄ 1999 Award Winner

Friesen, Gayle. *Janey's Girl.* Kids Can Press, 1998.

◄◄ 1998 Award Winner

Brooks, Martha. *Bone Dance*. Groundwood Books, 1997.

◄◄ 1997 Award Winner

MacIntyre, R. P., ed. *Takes: Stories for Young Adults.* Thistledown, 1996.

◄◄ 1996 Award Winner

Wynne-Jones, Tim. *The Maestro.* Orchard Books, 1996.

◄◄ 1995 Award Winner

Johnson, Julie. *Adam and Eve and Pinch Me.* Puffin Books, 1995.

⌒ *New Zealand Post Children's Book Awards*

In 1997 the *New Zealand Post* sponsored the Children's Book Festival. The awards were previously known as the AIM Children's Book Awards. The New Zealand Post Children's Book Awards recognize the best in New Zealand children's books.

▣ Junior Fiction

◂◂ 2000 Award Winner

Ford, Vince. *2MUCH4U*. Scholastic Incorporated, 1999.

◂◂ 1999 Award Winner

Cowley, Joy. *Starbright and the Dream Eater*. HarperCollins Children's Book Group, 2000.

◂◂ 1998 Award Winner

Cowley, Joy. *Ticket to the Sky Dance*. Viking Press, 1997.

◂◂ 1997 Award Winner

Lasenby, Jack. *The Battle of Pook Island.* Longacre, 1996.

◂◂ 1996 Award Winner

Lasenby, Jack. *The Waterfall.* Longacre, 1995.

▣ Nonfiction

◂◂ 2000 Award Winner

Te wao nui a Tane, ko nga waiata na HIRINI MELBOURNE; ko nga pikitia na TE MAARI GARDINER. Huia Publishers, 1999.

◂◂ 1999 Award Winner

Hutching, Gerard. *The Natural World of New Zealand*. Viking Press, 1998.

◂◂ 1998 Award Winner

Noonan, Diana. *The Know, Sow & Grow Kids Book of Plants.* Bridge Hill, 1997.

◂◂ 1997 Award Winner

Gaskin, Chris. *Picture Book Magic*. Reed Children's Books, 1996.

◄◄ 1996 Award Winner

Scown, Jenny. *Aya's Story*. Scholastic Incorporated, 1995.

▣ Best First Book

◄◄ 2000 Award Winner

Ford, Vince. *2MUCH4U*. Scholastic Incorporated, 1999.

◄◄ 1999 Award Winner

Erlbeck, Hana Hiriana. *Footsteps of the Gods*. Reed Children's Books, 1998.

◄◄ 1998 Award Winner

Knox, Judy. *Trapped*. Scholastic Incorporated, 1997.

◄◄ 1997 Award Winner

Westaway, Jane. *Reliable Friendly Girls*. Longacre, 1996.

◄◄ 1996 Award Winner

Ranger, Laura. *Laura's Poems*. Godwit, 1995.

∾ *Esther Glen Award*

Esther Glen was a New Zealand journalist, children's author, and book editor. This award, established in 1945, is given for the most distinguished contribution to New Zealand literature for children and young adults.

◄◄ 2000 Award Winner

No award given

◄◄ 1999 Award Winner

No award given

◄◄ 1998 Award Winner

Hill, David. *Fat, Four-Eyed and Useless*. Scholastic Incorporated, 1997.

◄◄ 1997 Award Winner

De Goldi, Kate. *Sanctuary*. Penguin Books, 1996.

◄◄ 1996 Award Winner

Marriott, Janice. *Crossroads.* Reed Children's Books, 1995.

D

Young Adult Books on Tape

Alcott, Louisa May. *Little Women.* Read by Rebecca Burns. 1,080 min.

Babbitt, Natalie. *The Search for Delicious.* Performed by the author and The Words Take Wing Repertory Company. 161 min.

———. *Tuck Everlasting.* Read by Peter Thomas. 211 min.

Banks, Lynn Reid. *The Indian in the Cupboard.* Read by the author. 262 min.

———. *The Return of the Indian.* Read by the author. 219 min.

Barrie, J. M. *Peter Pan.* Read by Donada Peters. 300 min.

Bensen, Michael. *Gloria Estefan.* Read by Marita DeLeon. 90 min.

Bodett, Tom. *Williwaw!* Read by the author. 335 min.

Burnett, Frances Hodgson. *The Secret Garden.* Read by Penelope Dellaporta. 540 min.

Burnford, Sheila. *The Incredible Journey.* Read by Megan Follows. 190 min.

Byars, Betsy. *Wanted . . . Mud Blossom.* Read by Blain Fairman. 199 min.

Christopher, Paul Curtis. *Bud, Not Buddy.* Read by James Avery. 360 min.

———. *The Watsons Go to Birmingham.* Read by LeVar Burton. 305 min.

Clements, Andrew. *Frindle.* Read by John Fleming. 99 min.

Cooper, Susan. *The Boggart.* Read by David Rintoul. 354 min.

———. *The Boggart and the Monster.* Read by David Rintoul. 284 min.

———. *The Dark Is Rising.* Read by Alex Jennings. 520 min.

Conly, Jane Leslie. *Crazy Lady.* Read by Ed Begley, Jr. 217 min.

———. *While No One Was Watching.* Read by Dylan Baker. 224 min.

Coville, Bruce. *Aliens Ate My Homework.* Read by William Dufris. 199 min.

———. *I Was a Sixth Grade Alien.* Read by William Dufris. 240 min.

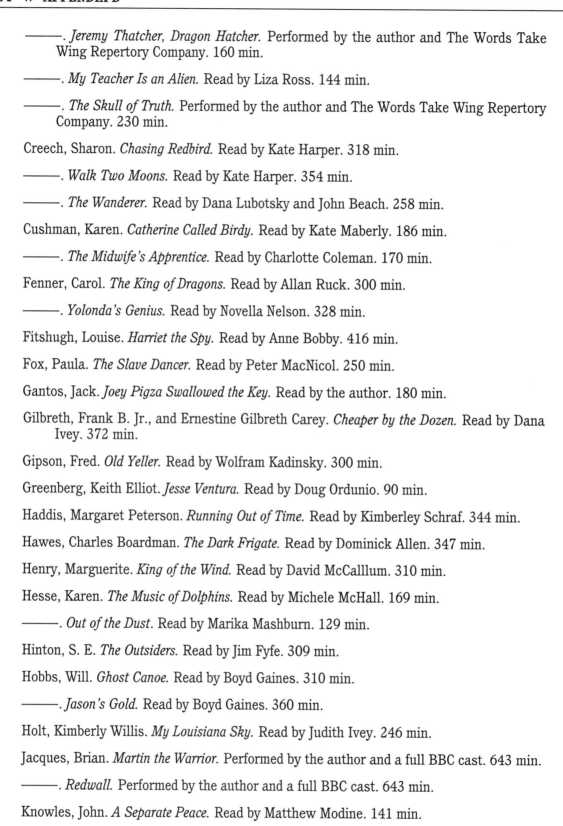

————. *Jeremy Thatcher, Dragon Hatcher.* Performed by the author and The Words Take Wing Repertory Company. 160 min.

————. *My Teacher Is an Alien.* Read by Liza Ross. 144 min.

————. *The Skull of Truth.* Performed by the author and The Words Take Wing Repertory Company. 230 min.

Creech, Sharon. *Chasing Redbird.* Read by Kate Harper. 318 min.

————. *Walk Two Moons.* Read by Kate Harper. 354 min.

————. *The Wanderer.* Read by Dana Lubotsky and John Beach. 258 min.

Cushman, Karen. *Catherine Called Birdy.* Read by Kate Maberly. 186 min.

————. *The Midwife's Apprentice.* Read by Charlotte Coleman. 170 min.

Fenner, Carol. *The King of Dragons.* Read by Allan Ruck. 300 min.

————. *Yolonda's Genius.* Read by Novella Nelson. 328 min.

Fitshugh, Louise. *Harriet the Spy.* Read by Anne Bobby. 416 min.

Fox, Paula. *The Slave Dancer.* Read by Peter MacNicol. 250 min.

Gantos, Jack. *Joey Pigza Swallowed the Key.* Read by the author. 180 min.

Gilbreth, Frank B. Jr., and Ernestine Gilbreth Carey. *Cheaper by the Dozen.* Read by Dana Ivey. 372 min.

Gipson, Fred. *Old Yeller.* Read by Wolfram Kadinsky. 300 min.

Greenberg, Keith Elliot. *Jesse Ventura.* Read by Doug Ordunio. 90 min.

Haddis, Margaret Peterson. *Running Out of Time.* Read by Kimberley Schraf. 344 min.

Hawes, Charles Boardman. *The Dark Frigate.* Read by Dominick Allen. 347 min.

Henry, Marguerite. *King of the Wind.* Read by David McCalllum. 310 min.

Hesse, Karen. *The Music of Dolphins.* Read by Michele McHall. 169 min.

————. *Out of the Dust.* Read by Marika Mashburn. 129 min.

Hinton, S. E. *The Outsiders.* Read by Jim Fyfe. 309 min.

Hobbs, Will. *Ghost Canoe.* Read by Boyd Gaines. 310 min.

————. *Jason's Gold.* Read by Boyd Gaines. 360 min.

Holt, Kimberly Willis. *My Louisiana Sky.* Read by Judith Ivey. 246 min.

Jacques, Brian. *Martin the Warrior.* Performed by the author and a full BBC cast. 643 min.

————. *Redwall.* Performed by the author and a full BBC cast. 643 min.

Knowles, John. *A Separate Peace.* Read by Matthew Modine. 141 min.

Konigsburg, E. L. *From the Mixed-Up Files of Mrs. Basil E. Frankweiler.* Read by Jan Miner. 220 min.

——. *The View from Saturday.* Read by Richard Adamson. 354 min.

Krohn, Katherine. *Princess Diana.* Read by Josephine Bailey. 90 min.

Lazo, Caroline. *Arthur Ashe.* Read by Ted Daniel. 90 min.

L'Engle, Madeleine. *A Swiftly Tilting Planet.* Read by the author. 464 min.

——. *A Wind in the Door.* Read by the author. 310 min.

——. *A Wrinkle in Time.* Read by the author. 345 min.

Levine, Gail Carson. *Dave at Night.* 330 min.

——. *Ella Enchanted.* Read by Eden Riegel. 354 min.

Lowry, Lois. *The Giver.* Read by Ron Rrifkin. 297 min.

Montgomery, L. M. *Anne of Green Gables.* Read by Rebecca Burns. 630 min.

——. *Anne of Montgomery.* Read by Megan Follows. 182 min.

——. *Anne of the Island.* Read by Megan Follows. 178 min.

Myers, Walter Dean. *Monster.* 180 min.

Naylor, Phyllis Reynolds. *Sang Spell.* Read by Ron Rifkin. 287 min.

——. *Saving Shiloh.* Read by Henry Leyva. 190 min.

——. *Shiloh.* Read by Peter MacNicol. 172 min.

——. *Shiloh Season.* Read by Michael Moriarty. 162 min.

North, Sterling. *Rascal.* Read by Jim Weiss. 281 min.

O'Dell, Scott. *Island of the Blue Dolphins.* Read by Tantoo Cardinal. 242 min.

Opdyke, Irene Gut, with Jennifer Armstrong. *In My Hands: Memories of a Holocaust Rescuer.* Read by Hope Davis. 433 min.

Paulsen, Gary. *Brian's Winter.* Read by Richard Thomas. 194 min.

——. *Brian's Return.* Read by Peter Coyote. 180 min.

——. *Canyons.* Read by Peter Coyote. 171 min.

——. *Hatchet.* Read by Peter Coyote. 229 min.

——. *The River.* Read by Richard Thomas. 155 min.

——. *The Soldier's Heart.* Read by George Wendt. 105 min.

——. *Woodsong.* Read by the author. 156 min.

Peck, Richard. *A Long Way from Chicago.* Read by Ron McLarty. 257 min.

Philbrick Rodman. *The Mighty.* Read by Elden Henson. 196 min.

Pullman, Philip. *The Golden Compass.* Performed by the author and a full cast. 649 min.

———. *The Subtle Knife.* Performed by the author and a full BBC cast, a Words Take Wing Production. 535 min.

Rawls, Wilson. *Where the Red Fern Grows.* Read by Anthony Heald. 397 min.

Richter, Conrad. *The Light in the Forest.* Read by Robert Sean Leonard. 175 min.

Roberts, Jeremy. *Saint Joan of Arc.* Read by Karen White. 90 min.

Rodgers, Mary. *Freaky Friday.* Read by Susannah Fellows. 201 min.

Rowling, J. K. *Harry Potter and the Chamber of Secrets.* Read by Jim Dale. 541 min.

———. *Harry Potter and the Goblet of Fire.* Read by Jim Dale. 1,140 mins.

———. *Harry Potter and the Prisoner of Azkaban.* Read by Jim Dale. 708 min.

———. *Harry Potter and the Sorcerer's Stone.* Read by Jim Dale. 541 min.

Rylant, Cynthia. *Children of Christmas and Every Living Thing.* Read by Sally Darling, Peter Thomas, Sucanne Toren, and Peter Waldren. 156 min.

———. *Missing May.* Read by Frances McDormand. 144 min.

Sachar, Louis. *Holes.* Read by Kerry Beyer. 270 min.

Siegel, Robert. *Whalesong.* Read by Don West. 180 min.

———. *When Zachary Beaver Came to Town.* 300 min.

Staples, Suzanne Fisher. *Dangerous Skies.* Read by Peter MacNicol. 325 min.

Taylor, Theodore. *The Cay.* Read by LeVar Burton. 171 min.

Tolkien, J. R. R. *The Hobbit.* Performed by a full BBC cast. 240 min.

Voigt, Cynthia. *Dicey's Song.* Read by Jodi Benson. 379 min.

Waiciechowska, Maia. *The Shadow of the Bull.* Read by Francisco Rivela. 214 min.

Wallace, Bill. *A Dog Called Kitty.* Read by L. J. Ganser. 179 min.

Walsh, Jill Paton. *A Parcel of Patterns.* Read by Brigit Forsyth. 285 min.

White, Ruth. *Belle Prater's Boy.* Read by Alison Elliott. 229 min.

Wolff, Virginia Euwer. *Bat 6.* Read by the author. 360 min.

E

Young Adult Literature Videos

(Suitable for Home or School Media Centers)

Armstrong, William A. *Sounder.* 1972. 105 min.

Banks, Lynne Reid. *The Indian in the Cupboard.* 1995. 98 min.

Byars, Betsy. *The Night Swimmers.* 1981. 46 min.

————. *The Summer of the Swans.* 1974. 45 min.

Cleaver, Vera and Bill. *Where the Lilies Bloom.* 1973. 97 min.

Dahl, Roald. *Matilda.* 1996. 86 min.

————. *The Witches.* 1989. 92 min.

Eames, David. *African Journey.* 1990. 174 min.

Forbes, Esther. *Johnny Tremain*, 1957. 80 min.

Gardiner, John Reynolds. *Stone Fox.* 1987. 96 min.

Hamilton, Virginia. *The House of Dies Drear.* 1988. 116 min.

Hickam, Homer H. Jr. *October Sky.* 1999. 108 min.

Juster, Norton. *The Phantom Tollbooth.* 1969. 89 min.

Konigsburg, E. L. *The Mixed-Up Files of Mrs. Basil. E. Frankweiler.* 1995. 92 min.

London, Jack. *White Fang*, 1991. 109 min.

Manes, Stephen. *How to Be a Perfect Person in Just Three Days.* 1983. 60 min.

Martin, David. *Clowning Around.* 1991. 176 min.

————. *Clowning Around II.* 1993. 176 min.

Naylor, Phyllis Reynolds. *Shiloh.* 1997. 93 min.

————. *Shiloh 2.* 1999. 96 min.

O'Dell, Scott. *The Island of the Blue Dolphins*. 1964. 99 min.

Paterson, Katherine. *Bridge to Terabithia.* 1985. 60 min.

———. *Jacob Have I Loved.* 1990. 57 min.

———. *Lyddie.* 1995. 90 min.

Philbrick, Rodman. *The Mighty.* 1998. 100 min.

Pinkwater, D. Manus. *The Hoboken Chicken Emergency.* 1984. 58 min.

Porter, Katherine Anne. *The Fig Tree.* 1990. 58 min.

Rawls, Wilson. *Summer of the Monkeys.* 1998. 101 min.

———. *Where the Red Fern Grows.* 1974. 97 min.

———. *Where the Red Fern Grows: Part Two.* 1991. 92 min.

Richter, Conrad. *The Light in the Forest.* 1958. 92 min.

Speare, Elizabeth George. *The Sign of the Beaver.* 1997. 100 min.

Spinelli, Jerry. *Maniac Magee.* 1992. 30 min.

Stevenson, Robert Louis. *Kidnapped.* 1960. 95 min.

———. *Treasure Island.* 1950. 96 min.

Taylor, Theodore. *The Cay.* 1990. 13 min.

Tolkein, J. R. R. *The Hobbit.* 1978. 78 min

———. *Return of the King.* 1980. 97 min.

Verne, Jules. *20,000 Leagues Under the Sea.* 1954. 127 min.

Wyss, Johann. *Swiss Family Robinson.* 1960. 126 min.